"Colonel Chamberlain, your gallantry was magnificent, and your coolness and skill saved us."

—Colonel James Rice
3rd Brigade Commander
1st Division
5th Corps

"I am very proud of the 20th Regiment and its Colonel. I did want to be with you and see your splendid conduct in the field. My heart yearns for you, and more and more now that these trying scenes convince me of your superiority. The pleasures I felt at the intelligence of your conduct yesterday is some recompense for all that I have suffered. God bless you and the dear old regiment."

—Brigadier General Adelbert Ames
11th Corps

In Search of Honor:

Rockland to Round Top

A narrative of Maine, Joshua L. Chamberlain, and the Twentieth Maine Regiment

As recollected by Benjamin Dean

BOOK ONE: MAINE

by Russell A. Dole

In Search of Honor

Copyright © 2018 by Russell Dole

All rights reserved. No part of this book may be reproduced or transmitted in any form or by any means without written permission of the author.

ISBN 978-1-943424-32-0

Library of Congress Control Number: 2018932840

North Country Press
Unity, Maine

Prologue

"Fix bayonets!" Hazy smoke and shot filled the air. The crack of gunfire followed by the hiss of minié balls passing over my head. Cries, groans, and heavy breathing mixed with sweat and pounding hearts. A sharp intake of breath, then, "Charge! Bayonets charge!" A movement of men to the left and the line swept forward like an unhinged gate toward the enemy advancing below.

The death this past winter of my dear friend and mentor Joshua L. Chamberlain and the recent stirrings of war in Europe have compelled me to take pen in hand and chronicle the decade leading up to that fateful day of July 2, 1863. Occurring over fifty years ago, the events of that steamy afternoon in southern Pennsylvania are still etched in my memory. Much has been written concerning the events of that day and controversy abounds. Who gave the command? Who led the charge? Who deserves the honor?

As a participant in and witness to that day's action I feel obliged to give my account and hopefully end the debate. Having the first-hand opportunity to witness the courage and leadership of the Twentieth Maine Regiment under such stalwart men as Holman Melcher, Ellis Spear, and Joshua Lawrence

Chamberlain, I feel a responsibility to do them justice and recount actions from my perspective and hopefully bring a resolution to the confusion and controversy.

The Twentieth Maine Regiment was a ragged and diverse collection of men hailing from all corners of Maine. Many like myself were from the coastal towns and cities stretching from York to Portland, eastward to the midcoast of Penobscot Bay and Rockland, up the Penobscot River to Bangor, and along the Down East shore through Mount Desert Island and Machias. Others came from the farming communities and woodlands of southern, central, and western Maine. Piscataquis and Aroostook counties produced volunteers from the Great North Woods extending north to the Canadian border. Farmers, woodsmen, fishermen, mariners, mechanics, merchants, clerks, and school teachers—we had no common ground. No county, city, or town claimed us as their own. We weren't volunteers from Knox or Cumberland counties, or volunteers from the capital of Augusta or town of Brunswick. We were simply Maine state volunteers.

No parades or fanfare sent us off to protect Washington, D.C. and do battle along the southern front surrounding the capital. No county or city flags gave us a common ground. The native stubbornness and the need for independence ingrained through our Yankee heritage made the transition from civilian life to military life difficult to overcome in the early months. Our first regimental commander Colonel Adelbert Ames, a West Point graduate from my hometown of Rockland, was appalled by our appearance and lack of military bearing. After one particularly discouraging performance in close order drill he declared, "This is a hell of a regiment!" He became so exasperated with our progress that he threatened to send us back from where we came. To his credit he persevered, molding us into the semblance of a military fighting unit. More importantly he recognized the calm presence and leadership potential of our Lieutenant Colonel, Joshua Lawrence Chamberlain.

Lawrence, as he was called by his family and close friends, was a thin man who appeared taller than his actual height of 5 feet 10 1/2 inches. A long face revealed light, gray-blue eyes and an almost prominent nose. During the war the growth of a full walrus-like mustache that almost obscured his mouth became a trademark. This dashing and stoic figure carried himself with an erect bearing and manner that made him look uncharacteristically military in comparison to the rest of the regiment. This charismatic man drew the regiment toward him, establishing a strong bond of faith and trust that was never questioned or challenged. This quiet, humble gentleman and scholar, of forthright character and determination, would lead our regiment to the greatest challenge we would face in our duty to the Union.

The narrative that follows traverses a decade of extraordinary change for me, my family, and my country, the United States of America. It begins when my forefathers first passed along the rocky shores of Penobscot Bay on the coast of Maine, where the tangy smell of the salt air mixes with the sweet smell of the pine forest. From the banks of the Penobscot River to the thick woods of the Allagash, to the halls of Bowdoin College to the bloody battlefields of Maryland, Virginia, and Pennsylvania, it was a decade filled with happiness, hope, and honor mingled with despair, doubt, and desperation. It begins at the place of my birth, where my character was forged and my ideals were nurtured. A place where my family gained success and earned the respect of the community by living and working with a sense of integrity, honesty, and compassion for their fellow men and women. It begins in a place called Rockland.

> Benjamin Dean
> Brunswick, Maine
> September, 1914

Rockland

Rockland is situated on the southwest entrance to Penobscot Bay about 75 miles north of Portland along Maine's mid coast. Its harbor, called Catawamteag ("Great Landing Place") by the local Indian tribes, lies between Owls Head to the south and Jameson Point to the north. North and west of Rockland rise the Camden Hills, where Dodge's Mountain, climbing to 558 feet, is closest to Rockland.

The Tarratine and Wawenock tribes were firmly established in the region when the first Europeans sailing with John Cabot may have skirted the coast in the late 1490s. In 1605, James Rossier, attached to the George Weymouth expedition, gave the first known English account of the inland region from aboard the ship *Archangel*. He described the river they navigated, christened the St. George, southwest of Penobscot Bay, the Camden Hills to the north, and the grassy meadows to the west. This expedition also sowed the seeds of discontent between the English and the local Indian tribes when an expeditionary crew of the *Archangel* captured a group of natives and attempted to abduct them as prizes for their return voyage to their king, James I, and their homeland. Tribal distrust of the English allowed rival

France to gain the upper hand in the region and made trade and colonization extremely difficult for the English over the next 100 years.

Later descriptions of the Penobscot Bay region came from Captain John Smith during his exploration and mapping of the New England coast and by French explorers led by Samuel De Champlain, the "Father of New France". Champlain may have been searching for the site of the legendary Norumbega, a jeweled city paved in gold. It is a legend similar to the tale of the Seven Cities of Cibola which the Spanish conquistador Francisco Coronado searched for in the southwest of North America in the previous century. Like the Spanish before them, neither the French nor the English who explored the Penobscot Bay ever discovered their El Dorado.

What they did discover was fish, and an abundance of it. As a result, an English foothold was finally established in the region about 1720 with the building of a blockhouse at the head of the peninsula along the banks of the St. George River. Named Fort St. George, it became a center of trade between the English and local Indian tribes. As trade increased the influx of English settlers into the region led to the first permanent settlement in the area, it would become known as Thomaston—the far eastern boundary of that site being the future location of

Rockland. As English settlement expanded in New England, conflicts with the French and their Indian allies developed and King George's War spread northward from southern New England to the Penobscot. A great threat to the English settlers along the Maine coast came from the French located to the northeast in nearby Acadia. In 1745 an expedition was sent north by Massachusetts governor William Shirley to protect its citizens along the Maine frontier. Their objective was the fortress at Louisburg on Cape Breton Island. Among the Massachusetts volunteers was my namesake and great, great, great-grandfather Benjamin Dean. His forefathers, hailing from the English seaport of Liverpool, had been among the first group of English colonists to settle Newbury, Massachusetts, about 1636. By 1745, Benjamin, closing in on thirty years of age, was drawn to the expedition by a sense of civic duty and a desire for one last adventure before assuming control of the family boatyard located near the mouth of the Parker River. A powerfully built man just over 5 and 1/2 feet tall, with light brown hair and hazel eyes, Benjamin, like the other members of the militia, hoped for a quick and exciting campaign in French Canada.

After the English victory over the French at Louisburg, Benjamin had the good fortune to sail and explore along Maine's mid coast upon his return to Massachusetts and became particularly interested in the region around Penobscot Bay. Impressed with the abundance of timber available and easy access to the coastal trade routes he returned to the area several times over the next two decades. Scouting timber stock for his flourishing boatyard, he developed a keen knowledge of the bay's geography, including its islands, and the river flowing in from the north. On many of these scouts around the shores of the bay and along the banks of the Penobscot River he was accompanied by his son Nathaniel, my great, great-grandfather.

Nathaniel's experiences along the Maine coast, on the rivers, and in the forests gave him a vast knowledge of the region. In 1775 this brought him a call from Colonel Benedict Arnold who was assembling an expedition to attack Quebec. Arnold and General George Washington planned a quick two-pronged invasion of Canada at the start of the American Revolution in the hopes of rallying "Les Habitants" to the American cause. Leaving Newburyport in the fall of 1775, the expedition moved up the coast to the mouth of the Kennebec River and paddled upstream through the heart of the Maine wilderness. They arrived on the southern bank of the St. Lawrence River as the Canadian winter set in. Battered and greatly diminished in size, the remnants of Arnold's army stormed the fortified walls of Quebec during a driving blizzard on New Year's Eve, 1775. The attack failed when Arnold was wounded at the onset and lacking leadership the Americans were hurled back. Those not captured, including Arnold and Nathaniel, retreated back to the southern bank of the St. Lawrence. Although the expedition failed to stop the British invasion from Canada the following year in 1776, it became legendary in the annals of war. After the harrowing experience of that campaign and another tour of duty under Arnold on Lake Champlain, Nathaniel made the decision to pull up stakes and leave Massachusetts for the tranquility of the Province of Maine. With his wife Rachel and their six children he guided his family northward to Maine.

In the year 1780 the Dean family established themselves on the shores of Penobscot at the northern end of Lermond's Cove. Built on the same stocky lines as his father Benjamin but with darker brown hair and brown eyes, Nathaniel worked hard to establish a boatyard in the recently settled area called Shore Village. An outgrowth of the earlier settlement of Thomaston, it was located five miles to the north and east. Shore Village had originally been settled in 1767 as a lumber camp and saw mill by John Lermond and his sons near what the Indians called "Catawamteag". During the early years it was commonly called Lermond's Cove and in its modest beginnings the settlement grew rapidly when the first permanent dwellings were built by Jonathan Crockett, Isaiah Tolman, and Ichabod Barrows. This natural harbor between Owls Head and Jameson Point was ideally suited for coastal trade and shipbuilding.

Although technically a part of Thomaston, Shore Village developed into an independent community. Farms and trading post were established and the names Rankin, Tilson, Berry, and Blackington became prominent. In the meadows west of the village limestone was found in abundance. Starting in 1785 the Ulmer family set up the first lime burning kiln at Lermond's Cove. This established a major industry that became the foundation of the settlement's early growth and continues to be a major economic base almost 130 years later.

Henry Knox, former Revolutionary War artillery general and the first Secretary of War in the Washington cabinet, retired to the Penobscot region in 1795. From Montpelier, his new mansion on the St. George River in Thomaston, he invested in the region's growing enterprises: limestone, lumber, and shipping. Although his business ventures proved unsuccessful, his presence and prestige enhanced the area's standing and business entered a boom era.

Rockland

The limestone and lumber industries created a need for schooners and coastal vessels to haul and market their products around and outside the mid coast area. This business climate enabled the Dean Boatyard to prosper and when my great-grandfather Samuel Dean took over the daily operations he expanded the business and changed the name to the Dean Shipyard in 1800. He hoped to call attention to the larger vessels being constructed there. To provide more diversity he opened a ship's chandlery. The new store sold grocery items, supplied salt and other goods for sea voyages, repaired ship parts, and provided services for the crews of the ships visiting the harbor. The business expansion thrived with the hard work and gregarious personality of Samuel.

Inheriting his height and dark features from his mother, a native of Maine, Samuel stood an inch over six feet with penetrating dark grey eyes and a full black beard. His outer appearance took on the look of a coastal buccaneer. With long rangy arms and legs he was an abundance of leverage and strength. Whether swinging an adz in the shipyard or an ax in the woods Samuel was a force to be reckoned with. Under this rough exterior was a man with a congenial nature, quick wit, and natural humor. These personal traits made him extremely popular with the local town folk as well as the sailors from away who constantly docked or anchored in the harbor. This popularity, coupled with his business sense, made him a huge success. As the shipbuilding industry thrived in the early 1800s a steady stream of ship's carpenters, ship smiths, joiners, plankers, sail makers, riggers and caulkers plied their trade at the shipyards around the harbor. The sound of broadaxes, saws, adzes, drills, and augers filled the air from Front Street to Atlantic Street every Monday through Saturday from 5:00 a.m. 'til 7:00 p.m. and beyond during the summer months.

The Embargo Act of 1807 and the subsequent War of 1812 brought an abrupt halt to the growth of the mercantile industries from the Penobscot south to the Chesapeake. Particularly hard hit by the British blockade were the coastal businesses in New England. To counteract the losses a sometimes profitable but dangerous coastal trade was established to run the blockade. From this enterprise Samuel, with the help of his oldest son Oliver, was able to keep the family business afloat. Oliver was Second Mate aboard the schooner *Oliver*, captained by William Spear, when the ship was overtaken by the British warship *Fly* in June of 1813. After being captured by the Royal Navy at the tender age of twenty-one, Oliver was transported to England where he spent fifteen months in the infamous Dartmoor Prison. Returning to America in the Fall of 1814, Oliver vowed never again to let the forces of tyranny stand in the path of liberty. His deep appreciation for all that Maine had to offer, especially the solitude of the Maine woods, can be attributed to his incarceration in that "hell hole".

My grandfather Oliver was short and stocky in stature, with brown hair and hazel eyes. After returning from England in 1814 he married my grandmother Martha Little, a lively and personable young lady from the nearby village of Goose Creek. Together they forged a partnership that lasted for forty-five years and was remarkable for the equality and flexibility it nurtured. The Treaty of Ghent later that December and the remarkable victory at New Orleans by General Andrew Jackson's forces in early 1815 over the British veterans of the Napoleonic Wars brought peace, nationalism, and respect to the United States. The maritime businesses that survived this era of hostility began the slow climb to prewar prosperity during the coming "Era of Good Feeling". Oliver, with his connection to the growing timber industry in northern Maine, helped to establish the Shore Village community as a major center of commercial activity along the shores of Penobscot Bay as the new decade began.

The 1820s were a time of major change at Shore Village. Maine, as part of the Missouri Compromise solution to the expansion of slavery west of the

Mississippi River, had gained its independence from Massachusetts and as the twenty-third state, entered the Union as a free state in 1820. A new meeting house was built in the village to accommodate the growing population and in 1824 a post office was established by David Crockett. This last event initiated a name change. Shore Village now became the town of East Thomaston. The quarrying of limestone about a mile west of the harbor began in earnest and lime-burning kilns, producing thick black smoke, dotted Lermond's Cove. The need for more coastal schooners to transport the lime south to commercial ports like Portland, Boston, and New York produced a flurry of shipyards on Front Street, just north of Lermond's Cove. A group of six yards, Bird; Cobb and Butler; Crockett; Dean; Kimball and Rhoades; and McLoon and Thomas competed for contracts and prime lumber floating down the Penobscot River from Bangor. The business of maneuvering and wheeling and dealing to obtain these contracts was ferocious at times and the connections my family established over the many years in business helped the Dean Shipyard to prosper near the top of the industry and withstand the competition. By the close of the 1820s, the growth of the limestone and shipbuilding industries, the establishment of a medical practice by Dr. James Merrill, a law office by Edwin S. Hovey, and the opening of Jeremiah Berry's Commercial House, a centrally located hotel and tavern, made East Thomaston the center of commercial activity along Penobscot Bay.

By the mid-1830s the region had fully recovered from the disastrous effects of the Embargo Act and the War of 1812. The Dean Shipyard and chandlery thrived in this expanded business climate and enjoyed bountiful growth. The quarrying, burning, and shipping of limestone brought about opportunities for new construction, repair, and servicing of a variety of ocean vessels. Bangor had become the premier river port for shipping lumber and the Penobscot River teemed with an abundance of schooners, windjammers, and barges cruising the shipping lanes up and down the Penobscot River and into Penobscot Bay, bringing added business into the harbors along the coast.

About this time my father Oliver Dean II began to take on a larger share of the responsibility for the daily operations of the shipyard and chandlery from my grandfather. Born in 1817, my father grew to just over six feet, with dark brown hair and eyes. A man with a quiet and reserved nature, he managed the chandlery but felt more at ease with the rough and tumble atmosphere of the shipyard. He especially enjoyed the solitude of the timber scouts that took him deep into the heart of the northern Maine woods and its vast abundance of prime timber.

On August 26, 1836, Oliver Dean II married Abigail Smith at the Congregational Church in East Thomaston. A Maine native, my mother's ancestors were among the first settlers of Thomaston. A strikingly beautiful lady, tall and slender, with blond hair and hazel eyes, it was from her that I first learned to read and enjoy the company of good books. For her times, gender, and region she was very well educated, versed in both French and Latin, with a thorough knowledge of the classics. Her natural ease at the art of mathematics and her outgoing personality made her indispensable in the daily operation of the chandlery. Her contribution to the success of the family business was only topped by her role as a loving wife and mother. Whether giving love and support to my father or tending to the daily needs of her three children, Samuel, born on April 24, 1837, Benjamin, born on January 16, 1839, and Carrie, born August 6, 1841, she was always the dominant presence in our lives.

In the spring of 1838 my grandparents left their home in the chandlery and moved into a log cabin they built on the eastern base of Dodge's Mountain. My parents and brother Samuel had been living temporarily in a small Cape Cod house on nearby Cedar Street and permanently relocated to the spacious living quarters atop the chandlery at the shipyard on Front Street. This location had a spectacular view of the harbor and Penobscot Bay to the east. It was here that my parents' family grew and prospered and where we called home.

The rising wealth, security, and peace along the Penobscot was briefly threatened by the outbreak of the Aroostook War during the winter of 1838 and 1839. Also known as the Northeast Boundary Dispute, the hostilities erupted over the uncertain border between Maine and Canada, particularly New Brunswick. With prime timber land at stake, lumbermen began arming themselves and threatening to forcibly remove any infringement on what they considered to be their rightful territory. The dispute became so heated that militia on both sides of the border were called up in anticipation of an all-out war. When Bangor and the Penobscot River looked threatened, my grandfather and father, both members of the local militia, sailed down east with a detachment of volunteer soldiers to the Maine border town of Machias.

Luckily for all concerned the federal government stepped in to relieve the tension before the conflict escalated into an all-out shooting war. General Winfield Scott, a veteran and hero of the War of 1812, was sent to Augusta in March of 1839 to work out a temporary truce with the help of the two contesting executives, Governor Fairfield of Maine and New Brunswick Governor Harvey. This action halted the hostilities and opened the way for final negotiations between the United States and Great Britain, the governing authority in Canada.

The American claim, based on the Treaty of Paris which officially ended the American Revolution in 1783, placed the southern boundary of the St. Lawrence River as Maine's northern boundary. After the War of 1812 the British claimed land as far south as the confluence of the Machias and Aroostook rivers. Finally in 1842, after three more years of threats and skirmishes, Daniel Webster, Secretary of State under President John Tyler, and the British representative Alexander Baring, First Lord Ashburton were able to reach a peaceful settlement. With the Webster-Ashburton Treaty, the boundary between the United States and Canada was established as following the St. John River in the north and the St. Croix River in the east.

With peace restored to the region the timber and shipbuilding industries entered into their most prosperous era. In East Thomaston, Hiram Berry, later a Civil War general killed at the Battle of Chancellorsville, established a lumber yard on Main Street near Lermond's Cove in 1845. The next year a five hundred foot commercial wharf was constructed at the end of Sea Street, jutting out into the harbor.

Rockland

In 1848 East Thomaston separated from Thomaston and on July 17, 1850, its name was changed to Rockland, recognizing in the words of later historian Cyrus Eaton, "since when the town, now a city, has rejoiced in its chosen name which when it is considered that its quarries of lime rock are the foundation on which prosperity of the place rests, all must acknowledge to be an appropriate one."

These were great times of joy and discovery for me. Born on January 16, 1839, I was at an age where summers became a mixture of work and play. By my tenth year I was stocking goods and running errands in the chandlery. In the shipyard I observed the carpenters, sail makers, plankers, and riggers as I carried their lumber, tarping, rope, nails, and caulking from station to station. The smell of salt air mixed with the smells of tar and fresh cut lumber from the yard was forever imbedded in my senses. During my free time I hiked the trails leading up to Dodge's Mountain and among the sweet scent of the pines I felt as one with the spirit of its name, Madambettox. The mountain overlooked Tolman Pond which was a favorite spot of mine for fishing, canoeing, and swimming. It had originally been named Madambettox by the local native tribe which literally means "great fish pond". It was renamed Tolman Pond when Isaiah Tolman settled nearby in 1769. In 1850 it was changed to Chickawauka Lake, "the place of smiling waters", a name most appropriate to my way of thinking.

Winters were spent learning my lessons from Mr. Osgood at the school house on Grove Street. After school I chopped firewood for our kitchen stove and kept the entrance of the chandlery clear of the mounds of snow which fell during many of our legendary winter storms, Nor'easters, that continuously battered our coastline with icy precipitation and heavy winds. Much of my later after school time was dedicated to my academics. My parents believed firmly in the need for a strong, well rounded education and made sure my brother, sister, and I spent many hours diligently studying and reading.

My brother Samuel, almost sixteen at the time, was being groomed to one day take over management of the shipyard and chandlery. Tall and lanky, with dark brown hair and eyes, his natural wit and intelligence all but assured him a happy and successful future at the Dean Shipyard. On the other hand, at five feet, seven inches, with a stocky build, hazel eyes, and light brown hair, my future looked certain to be outside the family business. In my fourteenth year, my mother envisioned a career for me in the ministry or in education. My father leaned toward a professional career for me in medicine, law, or as a military officer trained at West Point.

Personally, I looked for a simpler way of making a living: sailing a schooner, being a fisherman, or working as a hunter or logger in the woods. There were no lofty business or professional goals for my sister Carrie's future. At twelve years of age she had developed into the spitting image of our mother. She was a tall, thin young lady with long blond hair, dark green eyes, and a ruddy complexion. Casual in appearance and demeanor, she preferred the outdoor life to the more traditional domestic duties that were associated with most young ladies of her time. My parents felt that a strong primary education for Carrie in her projected role as a wife and mother was more than adequate. Carrie however had more lofty goals in her mind. A lover and excellent handler of animals, she was determined to further her education in the hopes of becoming a veterinarian.

Late in 1852 a severe Nor'easter slammed into the coast during our Christmas school break. Most of my vacation time was spent shoveling out the chandlery and shipyard as well as running messages through the six-foot-high snow drifts between the two locations. When we could get away from chores Samuel and I snowshoed to my grandparents' house out on Chickawauka for bowls of piping hot fish chowder and slices of fresh-baked bread still warm from the oven in the wood stove. The chowder, loaded with chunks of haddock, diced potatoes, and pan-fried onions in a creamy broth of milk and butter with a topping of bits of fried salt pork, warmed the body and satisfied the soul. It was a welcomed respite after our journey through the deep snow and freezing air. The bread, soft and chewy on the inside, with an outer crust that was hard and crispy was slathered with freshly-churned butter. The richness of the meal was fit for a king.

After our delicious repast refortified us and we had dug out the door yard for our grandparents, Samuel and I cleared snow from the small cove on nearby Chickawauka for a skating party and bonfire along the shore. It was during that gathering of old and new friends when my sister Carrie introduced me to her new friend Anne Holmes.

During the coming year my thoughts would be more and more occupied with Anne. Tall and thin, her long brown hair and large brown eyes, with long dark lashes and thick brows first attracted me. As our friendship developed it was her quick wit and compassion for others that endeared her to me. Personality, charm, intelligence, and beauty, she was my ideal.

The winter months of 1853 were unusually harsh but I was kept busy with a flurry of work and school activities. Our school master Mr. Osgood added a heavier academic load and Anne, Carrie, and I started a small reading circle. We introduced ourselves and other classmates to the new literature that had recently been published. Anne's compassion drew her to the controversial *Uncle Tom's Cabin* by Harriet Beecher Stowe. Carrie's favorite was *The Blithedale Romance* by Nathaniel Hawthorne. I enjoyed the Herman Melville adventure *Moby Dick*. Unknown to me at the time, that tale of danger, obsession, and strength would parallel events in my own life later on that year.

I also took two snow shoe trips ten miles inland for camping and ice fishing on Hobbs Pond and Alford Lake. On those trips my companion was Rockland's resident raconteur, philosopher, and jack-of-all-trades, Dexter Barrows, a legendary local character. Eight years my senior, he was like an older brother to me. His independence and carefree spirit were what drew me to his company.

He was born on the St. George Peninsula, south of Rockland, and his family had eked out a meager existence for generations as coastal fishermen, clam diggers, hunters, and trappers. Dexter had no formal education but liked to remind folks that his knowledge was acquired in the "school of life". An experienced coastal fisherman and boat builder, he was skillful with his hands and hired out at my father's shipyard when the need for work arose.

A man of naturally high intelligence and common sense, Dexter took me under his wing and added a wealth of woodsman craft to the skills taught by my father. On the other hand my attempts to improve Dexter's reading and writing skills were looked at with skepticism but tolerated. Trapping, hunting, and fishing were his main interests. Many times we returned from a hunting trip loaded with teal duck, pheasant, or a large white-tailed deer. Fishing trips with Dexter usually yielded an abundance of salmon or trout if we didn't fry up the entire catch at our campsite. Tall and lean, standing about six foot three, with wide shoulders, long, powerful arms, and large hands with long fingers, he later reminded me of that famous ax man from Illinois whose strength and character guided our country in its time of our greatest peril.

The spring thaw brought with it our infamous "mud season", where a walk out to the door yard could spell disaster. Ice outs began on the lakes and rivers, and activity increased outside in the shipyard. With school still in session and more responsibility at the shipyard, there was little free time to indulge myself with long walks with Anne or fishing trips with Dexter.

On May 22, 1853, a major disaster struck our home town when an enormous fire erupted, spreading through the downtown and destroying large blocks of the commercial district. This massive conflagration, forever known as the "Great Fire", started on Main Street at the Pillsbury Store, consuming the west side of the district blocks from Spring to Limerock Streets. Lost were the Rockland Hotel, the Commercial House, and most of the Shipbuilders Bank block.

On the east side of Main Street, the Berry Stables and the Dennis, Thorndike, and Young blocks were consumed. The community rallied as one to assist the volunteer fire department in an effort to douse the flames. Unfortunately, a series of misfortunes hampered all efforts. Two new fire engines, recently ordered, had not yet arrived. Low tide and a lack of water and pressure in the fire hydrants lessened the surge of water needed to drench the flames and soak down the buildings not yet involved. To add insult to injury a strong consistent wind gusting up to 35 knots made it difficult to contain the flames. When the smoke finally cleared, damage estimates ranging from $150,000 to $200,000 in property were lost. The emotional and financial toll to those directly involved were incalculable and a somber state of mind engulfed the whole community.

Shipyard Row was spared from direct devastation, but the aftermath was keenly felt by all the citizens of Rockland. Not only was an enormous amount of capital lost but the effort and commitment required to rebuild the commercial district took time and manpower away from the waterfront. These harsh realities hit me directly as I began my passage from childhood to young adulthood.

An immediate personal concern involving Anne and her family caused the disappearance of the joyful life I had always known. A sense of gloom and turmoil darkened what had once been anticipated as a bright future. The dry goods store Anne's father established the previous autumn was consumed by the fire and laid to waste. Losing the entire store's stock of goods and being a new business compounded the disaster and Mr. Holmes was now deeply in debt. Word spread around Rockland that he was going into a business partnership with his brother who ran a similar business in Brunswick. This would force the Holmes family to relocate fifty miles down the coast. To me it might as well have meant moving to the moon. The news hit me like a shot and left me angry and anxious. The chaos after the fire had left no time for socializing and as a result I had not seen Anne for nearly two weeks. When school finally resumed a week later, her chair was empty.

I needed to talk to Anne! I agonized for a week, feeling too awkward to visit her at home. Anne finally returned to school later that week and confirmed my worst fears—she and her family were returning to Brunswick. After school that day I walked Anne home to the house her family rented on Spring

Street. We walked in silence for the most part, only a few brief comments on how nice the weather had been and the controversy surrounding *Uncle Tom's Cabin*. Neither one of us wanted to initiate the dreaded topic of separation.

Our gloom was a complete contrast to the beautiful day that shown around us. It was the kind of early summer day that the people along the Maine coast look forward to after a cold, wet spring season. The sun was high and bright in the sky and a gentle and cooling onshore breeze, caused by the afternoon sea turn, was blowing in off Penobscot Bay. We reached the Holmes residence and stood at the front gate, silently gazing at one another, our eyes intently locked. I coughed uncomfortably, my head down barely able to utter a hushed goodbye. Anne took my hand in hers and kissed me gently on the cheek. We promised to write each other often and visit when time and distance could be overcome. We both knew it was not goodbye but until we meet again. She smiled as I turned to leave for home. Before rounding the corner on to Main Street I looked back, she was still standing at the gate. She waved, I waved back, rounded the corner and then she was out of sight. Heading north toward the shipyard, I thought about the approach of summer and the days beyond. Brunswick may have been only fifty miles away but from my young perspective it was on the other side of the universe.

School was recessed until early October, giving me a four-month break from my studies. At the end of the first week out of school the Holmes family departed for Brunswick. Among friends and neighbors gathered to see them off, Anne and I got a quick and very public last goodbye. She promised to write me as soon as they were settled into her grandparents' house near the Brunswick Mall on Maine Street.

To ease the burden of my heavy heart I plunged head first into my new duties at the shipyard. My father decided the time had come to learn the trades and crafts of shipbuilding and placed me in the new position of Shipbuilders Apprentice, putting behind me the previous role of "errand boy". This was just one more indication that my days of carefree childhood were over. My new responsibilities placed me under the direct supervision of Dexter Barrows who had been hired full time by my father. It was the first time I could remember Dexter keeping steady work, another indication that life was changing. Always skilled and versatile, Dexter became a model employee, on time, always on the job, and willing to dive into any task asked of him. Dexter's change of direction in his life was in his own words a means to get respectable and become an established citizen within the Rockland community.

I suspected that his motives to get respectable were centered around his recent encounter with the blossoming Miss Lucy Farnsworth, a young lady who came from one of Rockland's most established and prominent families. Her father William owned a general store on Elm Street and was also a partner in the recently established Rockland Water Company. The new enterprise had tapped the fresh water source of Chickawauka by laying pipe from the lake to the downtown business district. His position in the community and Lucy's recent coming of age and introduction to Dexter had changed his life's view. It was the first time in my memory that his vision looked to the promise of the future instead of the needs of the immediate present.

Among adzes, broadaxes, augers, jacks, and clamps my knowledge of shipbuilding progressed steadily that summer under Dexter's watchful eye. Acquiring the drive and ambition that had previously been absent, Dexter became a true master of his craft. An expert "liner up", he taught me the fine art of lining up a vessel, taking a "spiling" or plug for each plank, and making a correctly-beveled caulking seam water tight. By summer's end I was proficient enough to be part of a steady work crew.

In Search of Honor

The long summer hours from 5:00 a.m. to 7:00 p.m. left little time for idleness. It was just the right medicine needed to keep my mind from wandering and constantly thinking of Anne. I received three letters from her over the course of the summer and had written back to her twice. She tried to put up a positive front in her letters but her loneliness for her friends in Rockland could not be easily masked. When writing her I mentioned the approaching fall school term and the hope of her renewing old friendships in Brunswick. I also told her that I longed for the day when she and I could be together again. Little did I know at the time that our reunion would be longer in coming and the time in between filled with more heartbreak and turmoil than either one of us could have imagined.

In late August my father announced that he was going as far north as Chamberlain Lake on a timber scout. To my surprise and excitement he asked Dexter and me to be his traveling companions. My father was an excellent judge of timber and much sought after by the lumber companies to work as a "cruiser". His job would be to survey the tracts of timberland to be harvested and estimate the number of thousands of board feet available using calipers for measuring. Hiram Berry, a local businessman and politician, was the owner of the largest lumber yard along Penobscot Bay and had asked my father

Rockland

to scout and survey lumber for the upcoming cutting season. Dexter and I were brought along to assist him in the woods and help with the canoe paddling along the various water routes we would travel.

My father's plan was to leave Rockland in mid-September and travel by schooner up the Penobscot River to Bangor. Although most of our time would be spent traveling or scouting and measuring timber, a chance to go into the north woods was like a vacation. It would also provide a positive ending to an emotionally difficult summer recess before resuming school in mid-October. The next two weeks couldn't fly by fast enough!

At 5:00 a.m. on September 14th, my father, Dexter, and I boarded a northbound steamer outside Rockland harbor and proceeded up the bay toward the river. Our destination was the Chamberlain farm in Brewer situated east across the Penobscot River from Bangor. The early morning sun was rising over the bay from the east and radiating its brilliance across the waters of the Penobscot. On the steamer *Penobscot* we rounded Jameson Point and headed north, gliding slowly in the center of the West Bay channel. On its weekly run from Boston to Bangor its black hull and white deck shone brightly in the early morning sunlight. Out beyond the bow of the steamer the islands of Vinalhaven and Northhaven emerged into view. With warm late summer weather and visibility of five to seven miles our six-hour voyage promised to be pleasant and relaxing. Passing Clam Cove the Camden Hills came into view, sparkling like a dark blue onyx in the west. Coming up on the mouth of the Goose River flowing into Goose Harbor, Rockport Village was beginning to come alive with the bustle of early morning activity. As the morning sun peered over Beaucamp Point, we cruised around Headman's Point coming up to Negro Island located on the eastern edge of Camden Harbor where the waters of the Megunticook River empty and Mount Battie, just inland, towers above.

As we passed by Sherman's Point, Islesboro came into view. Situated about three miles east of the mainland, the island was teeming with activity as the local fishermen and lobstermen plied their nets and traps to secure their daily catch. On we glided, past Duck Trap Stream, Saturday Cove at Northport, and a mile and a half to the east, Turtlehead, where the northern tip of Islesboro was on the starboard beam.

Further north was Belfast Bay where the Passagassawakeag River emptied, around Mack Point and into Long Cove, for years home of the ship captains' village of Searsport. As we approached Sears Island we were at the halfway point with about three hours of travel before us. Finally, we sighted the head of the bay at Fort Point where the surviving remnants of Fort Pownall, built almost one hundred years earlier as protection for the English settlements during the French and Indian War, could still be clearly discerned from the water's edge. Passing Sandy Point we arrived at the mouth of the Penobscot River.

    The river's mouth is divided into an east and west channel by Verona Island. We took the west channel and headed for the Narrows, a passage at the northern end of the island. As we cruised through the Narrows, the river town of Bucksport hugged the east bank and hovering above us on the west bank were the massive granite walls of Fort Knox.

    The fort had been brought under construction as a reaction to the Aroostook War, a brief and limited conflict between Maine and Canadian lumbermen over timber rights in the northern Maine woods. With the threat of British intervention and possible attack upriver on Bangor, a vital center for the Maine lumber industry, the plan to build a fort at the mouth of the Penobscot River as protection went into action. Named for General Henry Knox, the Revolutionary War hero and first Secretary of War under general and president George Washington, the fort was an enigma. The Webster-Ashburton Treaty between the United States and Great Britain had resolved the conflict, leaving the need for the fort obsolete and a great waste of money. As we passed the fort it was still under construction, years after the first huge slabs of granite had been laid for its foundation and walls. Seventy-five years later it has not been completed or fully utilized as a military installation.

The granite used to construct the fort was hauled downriver from Mount Waldo. We caught our first glimpse of that high peak as we left the Narrows and continued north of Bucksport. Five hours of travel put us abreast of Marsh Bay, with Waldo towering above us on the western bank. Around the bend of the river we came past the Frankfort shipyard, and in half an hour we had reached Winterport, the head of winter navigation on the river. Across the river on the east bank were the farms and fields of Orrington, upriver to Hampden and the highlands on the west bank before finally docking on the east bank at our destination, Brewer.

We disembarked at noon. There to meet us was a long-time friend of my father's, Joshua Chamberlain. Standing tall and erect, with dark eyes and a heavy dark beard, his military bearing revealed a no-nonsense approach to daily life. Although he was about fifteen years older than my father, they had developed a mutual respect for one another over a decade of time. They had first crossed paths in 1839 in Eastport during the Aroostook War where Mr. Chamberlain commanded the militia my father served as a volunteer. Since those days they had collaborated often as Mr. Chamberlain, like my father, was highly regarded as an expert judge of timber. It was because of this relationship that we disembarked on the Brewer side of the Penobscot. My father was interested in obtaining the best and latest first-hand information concerning the northern timber land and Mr. Chamberlain had made a trek north the previous month.

After a brief and formal introduction by my father, Mr. Chamberlain led us from the riverfront landing to his waiting wagon and team of two huge Clydesdale horses. Sitting in the driver's seat manning the reins was a tall, thin solemn-looking younger version of Mr. Chamberlain who I judged to be in his mid-twenties. He and my father exchanged greetings, shook hands, and then Dexter and I were introduced to Lawrence. This was my first meeting with the man who would have a positive and profound effect on my life for many decades. Although later known as Joshua Lawrence Chamberlain in his public life, his given name was Lawrence Joshua Chamberlain. He was named after a great naval hero of the War of 1812, Captain James Lawrence, who was mortally wounded in June of 1813. Commanding the *USS Chesapeake*, Lawrence is best known for having uttered the famous phrase "Don't give up the ship!" as he lay dying on the ship's deck. Joshua, the name Chamberlain is most commonly known as, was the name of both his grandfather and father. To his family and friends he was always known as Lawrence. Like his father he assumed the same military bearing, standing tall and erect, but with less of the austere presence that his father projected. Unlike his father, Lawrence's dark eyes were animated and sparkled when he first spoke with us.

After a short wagon ride we arrived at the Chamberlain farm, a 100-acre plot on the quiet east bank of the Penobscot. On the opposite bank sat Bangor, crowded, noisy, and bustling with activity in the midday sun. After refreshing ourselves at the water pump we were served a sumptuous noontime meal of corned beef, boiled potatoes and carrots, pickled beets, warm baking powder biscuits, fresh creamy butter, and cold milk to wash it all down. We topped off that delicious feast with Maine blueberry pie and more cold milk. Our gracious host was the kindly family matriarch Sarah Chamberlain, affectionately called Sally by those closest to her. Where father Joshua was silent, stern, and military, mother Sally was just the opposite, full of life and laughter. A deeply religious person, Sally was the anchor of the family. During the meal we became acquainted with the rest of Lawrence's siblings, Horace, Sarah, John, and Thomas. John and Tom

Rockland

were closest to my age and we hit it off right from the start.

After meal time my father and Mr. Chamberlain crossed the river to conduct business and finalize our travel plans in Bangor. Dexter and I followed the Chamberlain boys to the south field where we pitched in to help with the early fall haying. During the warm afternoon's work I learned more about Lawrence, the obvious leader and model for the younger Chamberlain brothers. He had just turned twenty-five on September 8th. In his early years he had developed an interest in boats, music, and the northern Maine woods, especially the native lore he had learned while visiting the Penobscot Indian village located on Indian Island in the middle of the Penobscot River, about five miles north of Bangor. His father hoped he would pursue a military career and sent him Downeast to the town of Ellsworth where he attended Major Whiting's Military Academy. There he learned military drill and studied Latin and French. The latter studies eventually led him south to Bowdoin College in Brunswick where he excelled at languages and graduated Phi Beta Kappa in 1852. His goal was to become a missionary, satisfying his own adventurous spirit and his dear mother's desire for him to enter the clergy and serve God. The past year had been a busy one for Lawrence. After graduating from Bowdoin he entered the Bangor Theological Seminary to further his religious studies. As a member of the Congregational Church in Brewer, Lawrence directed the choir, played the church organ, and taught Sunday School. He also acted as an interpreter for his father and the French Canadian Habitants when his father's timber scouting took him north of the border in the early spring that year. During that trip father and son snowshoed from Brewer on the Penobscot River to Rimouski on the St. Lawrence River.

After the chores were finished and a light evening meal of fresh fruit, corn muffins, and more fresh, cold milk was consumed we bade goodnight. We needed to get an early start in the morning to cross the river and catch the stagecoach from Bangor to Greenville and Moosehead Lake. Awake before sunrise we were treated to a hearty breakfast of bacon, eggs, pan-fried potatoes, homemade bread and jam by our gracious hostess, all washed down with two cups of piping hot and strong black coffee.

The sun was rising in the east when we gave our thanks to the Chamberlains and bade our farewells at the river's east bank. Lawrence ferried us across the Penobscot in the family sloop *Lapwing* and at the western bank we parted company. Although I had only met him the previous day, Lawrence's presence and character had made a great impression on me.

That point of view toward him has lasted for over sixty years!

In 1853 Bangor was known as the lumber capital of the world. Hundreds of thousands of logs floated down the east and west branches of the Penobscot to the sawmills in Old Town and Orono just upriver from Bangor. After sawing was completed coastal schooners were loaded, transporting millions of board feet of lumber from Bangor down the eastern seaboard and beyond the shores of the United States.

As we walked through the "Devil's Half Acre", a section of the city between Washington, Exchange, and Bangor streets, dark clouds rapidly moved in to hide the sun and a light rain began to fall. This section of the city was the home of the "Bangor Tigers", the lumbermen and river drivers who frequented the area during their months away from the Maine woods. Notorious for its taverns, grog shops, flop houses, brothels, and rowdy atmosphere, it seemed calm and quiet during this early morning hour. Walking up Hammond Street we reached the intersection of Union Street and the Bangor Theological Seminary where Joshua Chamberlain was studying for the clergy. Hiking up Union Street we passed the stately homes of the lumber barons, those men who controlled the vast tracts of land in the forests to the north. We reached the Bangor

House and made arrangements for the stagecoach to Greenville. As we approached our transportation, the driver was securing a birch bark canoe to the roof. Standing next to the stage watching the driver were three men. One of them stepped from the group and hailed us, "Hello gentlemen and welcome, I'm Henry David Thoreau."

Thoreau was of average height, with blue-gray eyes, dark hair, and a prominent aquiline nose. His slender torso was set upon a set of spidery legs. He seemed a friendly and outgoing sort as he chatted on amicably about the coming journey and the sights we would encounter. In contrast, his two companions, Thoreau's distant cousin, and their Penobscot Indian guide Joe Aitteon, barely uttered a word to our group. My father had been quite curt and formal during the introductions. I found out later that unlike Dexter and I, my father was familiar with Mr. Thoreau. His reputation had preceded him as a dissenter with the publication of his work "Civil Disobedience" in 1849. This dissertation described Thoreau's refusal to pay taxes as a protest against the Mexican War. My father had great disdain for those who went against the laws of our society. He believed these acts of rebellion disrupted order and had a negative impact on Americans in general. Thoreau did not seem to notice or at least did not mind my father's coolness as he rambled on about the fauna and flora of Maine.

At seven that morning, with our bags stowed away, we all crowded into the coach, my father, Dexter, and I on one bench, and opposite us was Thoreau and his cousin. The Penobscot guide Aitteon rode atop the stage with the canoe.

The crack of the whip signaled our start and we headed west out of Bangor on the Avenue Road for the next leg of our journey north and west to Greenville and the open expanse of Moosehead Lake, gateway to the Maine wilderness.

In the Maine Woods

We had seventy miles of travel from Bangor to Greenville. With scheduled rest stops totaling ten hours, the journey to Moosehead Lake would end about mid-morning the following day. As we reached the outskirts of Bangor our traveling companion Thoreau was in fine spirits. His descriptions of the forest trees ranged from "magnificent spruce tops" to "wild fir", "ball-spruce", "fir balsam", and "arbor vitae" delivered with gusto and enthusiasm. Taking a deep breath he proclaimed the odor of the evergreens "the sweet aroma of Maine!"

Early in our trip he informed us that this was his second excursion into the Maine woods. In 1846 Thoreau and two companions had traveled up the Penobscot River, hiking overland to Maine's highest summit, Mt. Ktaadn. After climbing up 5,000 feet to its peak he and his party descended down to follow the West Branch of the Penobscot River back to Bangor. On this trip he planned to travel the waterways of the Maine wilderness starting with a canoe ride up Moosehead Lake.

As we moved out of the Penobscot River Valley the terrain became quite level over the next twenty-five to thirty miles, increasing our speed. Thoreau mentioned he had heard on good authority that a traveler along this route in clear weather would have frequent views of Mt. Ktaadn about seventy-five miles due north and it was unfortunate that the low-lying clouds and heavy mist obscured that opportunity. Despite the rainy weather the road we traveled was quite firm and very smooth. We passed through a mixture of forests and open fields with very little land under cultivation. The houses along the roadside were mostly small Cape Cods, few and far apart. As we drifted farther north log cabins began to appear more frequently, indicating our entrance into the wilderness region. Thoreau became very intrigued by the long water troughs that were seen along the roadside. He thought it was a grand idea that the state paid out three dollars annually to one man in each school district to maintain a supply of fresh water to travelers and their animals.

After stopping for water about thirty miles northwest of Bangor the land began to rise abruptly, the road consisting of steep hills which slowed our progress. Mountains could be seen in the surrounding area. Around mid-afternoon we stopped in Sangerville to warm and rest ourselves at the local inn and feed, water and rest the coach horses.

Dexter proclaimed to the proprietor that he was so hungry he could eat "a whole side of beef, a bushel barrel of potatoes, and a row of corn on the cob drenched in butter and washed down with a keg of hard cider!" Like the rest of us he settled for a bowl of venison stew, a bit greasy but chock full of potatoes and carrots which produced quite a tasty broth. Biscuits with butter were used to sop up the broth left at the bottom of the bowl.

During the afternoon meal Thoreau kept up a running monologue on topics ranging from the beauty of wildflowers to the portaging of a canoe. All the while his arms and hands were flopping in various directions. His conversation was excitable and full of all sorts of detailed knowledge. He described "the handsome mountain ash with its vibrant colors and the hobble bush with its ripe berries of purple and red". On portaging he explained turning the canoe and lifting it with the bottom side up, the canoe man setting her over his right shoulder and ready to walk away. Our repast and cultural lesson completed, we resumed our trip in weather that had turned raw and rainy.

With evening approaching pockets of fog blanketed our route, bringing on the darkness faster than usual and slowing our progress. Twenty miles from Sangerville we reached the fork in the road between Abbott and Monson. A pair of moose horns serving as a sign post directed us to take the right fork to Monson, about seven miles north. We were only twenty miles from Moosehead Lake!

In Search of Honor

Arriving in Monson well after dark, cold and damp, our party headed quickly to the roadhouse for warmth and a hot meal. Inside the owners, a husband and wife, had built a roaring fire that filled the tap room with welcomed heat and the odor of burning pine. We dried and warmed ourselves in front of the fireplace until the stage coach hands came through the doorway. A long table with benches on either side had been set out in the center of the room with a drinking mug, large bowl, and eating utensils at each place setting.

The husband and wife worked well as a team to make us feel as welcomed and comfortable as possible. The crackling fire, its orange and blue flames shooting up the chimney, brought forth a feeling of coziness throughout the small room. In this hospitable atmosphere we supped on fresh brook trout, pan fried potatoes, a leg of roast mutton, corn on the cob dripping with melted butter, and a freshly baked loaf of sourdough bread. Strong black coffee was served during the meal and after to compliment the finishing touch, a warm apple crisp. Its flaky crust and sweet apple slices ended our repast in grand style.

As had been the case during the noon meal, Thoreau dominated the evening meal conversation. His topics ranged from his climb of Mt. Ktaadn during his '46 trip to Maine to "gearing up" for a journey such as this into the Maine woods. Speaking of Ktaadn he recalled "standing atop that spacious table-land with a view that took one's breath away". He described countless lakes, Moosehead to the southwest, "like a gleaming silver platter!", Chesuncook to the west, "long and narrow, without an island", Millinocket to the south, "with its hundreds of small islands", many numerous lakes without a name, and mountains, "whose names are known only to the Indians".

After the main meal was finished and coffee and crisp were being consumed, Thoreau continued his conversation by shifting direction and emphasizing the importance of good outfitting when traveling through the Maine woods. He suggested wearing a heavy check shirt, stout shoes, thick socks, rugged trousers, a bandana and a wide-brimmed felt hat. As he spoke I noticed he was already dressed for his travels.

He went on to give a detailed list of essentials needed to insure a successful completion of a wilderness trip. Always carry an India rubber knapsack with a large top flap for storing a change of clothes, needles, thread, pins, and a seven-foot-long gray blanket. Bring along a six by seven by four-foot-high canvas tent. Carry insect wash or soap, a pocket map, compass, jack knife, an ax, fish lines, hooks, two large pieces of soap, and utensils for cooking and eating.

As for provisions to supplement food gathered, hunted, or fished, he recommended hard bread, pork in an open keg, sugar, black tea, coffee, a box of salt, Indian cornmeal for frying fish, lemons for boiling water, and rice for variety. All provisions should be packed into two large water-tight India rubber bags. As he was winding down his dissertation Dexter quietly mentioned Thoreau's trip was built for comfort, not speed! To conclude Thoreau indicated the above-mentioned outfitting would cost at least twenty-four dollars, a large expense, but he also noted emphatically "worth every penny!"

It was after 10:00 p.m. when our meal and "lecture" were concluded. My father, Dexter, and I headed out to the stables to catch a few hours of shut-eye in the hayloft before the stage departed at 4:00 a.m. on the final leg of our journey to Greenville. My father, wanting to avoid Thoreau's company for the remainder of the night, steered Dexter and me to the opposite hayloft. Thoreau didn't miss a beat continuing his commentary with his party and the stage crew.

Under his breath Dexter declared Thoreau was a "jabbering fool jaybird" who was harder to swallow than "Grandma McBirney's Mystery Tonic"! My father did not utter a word but his facial expression indicated a strong agreement with Dexter's comment. As for myself I was rather indifferent to the whole situation. At that point all I desired was to lie down in the softness of the hayloft and sleep. A full belly coupled with the warmth of that small roadhouse room had done me in. I settled into my bedroll and let my sleepiness carry me away. As I drifted off into the throes of dreamland the faint sounds of an animated conversation were still audible across the other side of the stable. Even at this hour after a very long and tiresome day Thoreau was still holding court!

At 4:00 a.m. the following morning the stagecoach pulled out of the Monson roadhouse and we were on our way to Moosehead Lake. The rain of the previous evening had slackened to a fine mist but the muddy road, coupled with the early morning darkness and fog considerably slowed our progress north. Our traveling party had taken on an additional passenger who occupied the bench opposite us, sitting next to Thoreau. I had noticed him seated alone at a small corner table in the roadhouse the previous evening. He watched with interest as Thoreau regaled us at the dinner table but remained silent throughout the course of the evening before quietly retiring about an hour before our group headed for the stables.

In Search of Honor

I had forgotten about him after we turned in the previous evening and his appearance the following morning as we boarded the stagecoach surprised me. He was very tall, about 6 feet 4 inches, well-proportioned with broad shoulders, with long arms and legs. Unlike the average male traveler in this part of Maine he was dressed like a gentleman. Atop his massive head sat a black, wide-brimmed, silk hat. He wore a dark black long coat, with a necktie cravat and white shirt trimmed with black lace.

His trousers were dark gray with black piping along the seams and his black knee-length boots were highly polished. He carried an oak cane with silver tip at the bottom and his refined manner was an oddity among his fellow travelers.

His dark complexion contrasted sharply with his fine white teeth and this created an appearance of smarminess that aroused my suspicions as we were being introduced. A thick mane of black hair, bushy eyebrows, and well-trimmed goatee added to the effect. As usual Thoreau was the first of us to engage the stranger who explained that he was returning to his home in Quebec City after a business trip south to New York City. He introduced himself as Jean Raymond Brisebois.

Brisebois intrigued me. Extremely well dressed and cultivated he wasn't the typical traveler in the backwoods of Maine. The question "why us?" stayed with me for a long time and after ten painful years of searching, many of the answers I was seeking were uncovered. The dark cloud that descended on my family that day changed our lives forever and that scouting trip into the Maine woods altered my world view from that day forward.

He came from the lowland country of South Carolina. His ancestors, French Huguenots, had fled to the English North American colonies in 1685 after the revocation of the Edict of Nantes which had granted rights and protection to Protestants living in Catholic France. Developing an enormous rice plantation twenty-five miles north of Charleston on the Ashley River, the Brisebois family had prospered for generations. Like the Laurens and Legarés of their region, the Brisebois family was associated with the genteel lifestyle of the southern planter class. He explained he had arrived in Portland and was on his way to Quebec City in an attempt to expand his family's business interests north of the border. He was traveling through Maine with the idea that Portland would provide a direct link between the states and Canada.

The stagecoach ride from Monson to Greenville was uneventful. All of us except Thoreau used the time to resume our slumbers. From the early morning darkness through the foggy dawn Thoreau kept a running commentary on flora, fauna, and celestial observations to a less than captive audience. Finally, after five and a half hours on the road the driver called back that we were approaching the overlooking crest of Indian Hill. Looking through the front of the carriage's side windows we caught our first glimpse of Moosehead Lake about a mile down below the crest. Through the mist and morning light Moosehead looked like an enormous sparkling jewel before us. At the southern tip of the lake lay our destination, the village of Greenville.

Reaching the base of the hill the driver slowed the pace of the horses as we entered the village and steered the carriage into the door yard of the stage depot. As we slowed to a stop my father opened the door and was out of the coach as if he had been shot out of a cannon. In an agitated voice he summoned for Dexter and me to follow suit immediately. As we were gathering our gear from the stage my father tipped and thanked the driver, gave a nod and short, curt goodbye to our traveling companions, and turned heel, swiftly walking away. Dexter and I, with some confusion, bid all adieu, turned, and ran down the main street of Greenville to catch up with my father. Two blocks away, still walking at a brisk pace and in silence, we came to the office of Mr. Rockwood, Greenville lumber agent and inspector for the Penobscot River Lumber Company.

In the Maine Woods

While we waited outside as my father made arrangements with Mr. Rockwood, Dexter wondered when we were going to stop and eat something or if my father might make us paddle all the way up to the lake's northern shore and our destination, Northeast Carry. In describing my father's quick departure from the stage depot, Dexter indicated "he looked like a man heading for a fire." Looking around uncomfortably I whispered that I thought our traveling companions, particularly Mr. Thoreau, had put my father's nerves over the edge.

My father appeared from Mr. Rockwood's office and again without a word we headed straight for the lumber company's dock near the town landing. It was now ten o'clock and the sun had finally burned through the morning mist. Looking out across the lake from the southern shore of Moosehead the view to the north was a spectacular sight. The sun's rays glittered over the expanse of Moosehead's waters in contrast with the dark and dense green forest that blanketed the shoreline. Awaiting us at the dock was a twelve-foot birch bark canoe with three paddles. My father directed us in the loading of our gear and organized the seating order for the journey north.

We shoved off from the dock and headed into the wide open water with me in the bow, Dexter at midships and my father in the stern. In spite of the abundant sunshine a steady breeze out of the northwest kept a chill in the air and our voyage was a cool but comfortable one. Our birch bark canoe carried us north along the lake's western shore. The water at that time of the day was fairly calm which allowed us to paddle about a quarter of a mile from the shoreline. My father, an experienced canoeist, wanted me to keep a watchful eye ahead to spot white caps from the bow. The winds on Moosehead generally blow from the north and would increase in speed as the day progressed. We would not only be fighting a stiff headwind of up to twenty-plus knots later in the day but also combating choppy water and the threat of capsizing as the waves increased with the intensity of the winds.

As we paddled north and visibility improved we began to observe a variety of activities along the immediate shoreline and on the lake. A red fox was ripping apart a small creature at the water's edge. Was it fish or fowl?

At the confluence of one of the many brooks feeding into Moosehead, deer—two does and three lambs, their coats gleaming in the late morning sun—were helping themselves to the abundant grass and drinking from the brook's icy cold water. As we glided by the brook one of the mother deer abruptly raised her head, her nose dripping with water, she sniffed the air and her ears began to twitch as she sensed potential danger. At that point we spotted the height of Squaw Mountain, the source of the numerous brooks that fed into the lake. Further up the shoreline a huge bull moose, about ten yards off the shore, was feeding on lily pads in the shallow water. His head partially submerged displayed a huge rack of horns and his attention was so focused on his meal that he paid us no heed as we closely glided past.

By this time the sun had moved around the lake to the south and shade began to overtake the western shoreline. Numerous ripples in the water announced the presence of fish stirring below the surface in anticipation of their noontime feeding. As my father and I continued to paddle up the lake, Dexter, a top-notch angler, cast a line into the water to snag a catch as a tasty supplement to our approaching midday meal. Anticipating a feast of trout my mouth watered at the thought of their golden goodness. My father had been so determined to distance us from our traveling companions when we arrived in Greenville that, with the exception of a handful of dried fruit and water from the canteen, we had not had a substantial meal since our dinner in Monson the previous evening.

As usual Dexter's expertise with a fishing line had resulted in a fine catch of six large lake trout ranging in size from ten to twenty inches. Approaching Deer Island near the outlet to the Kennebec River we paddled ashore. After securing the canoe Dexter commenced to clean the trout while my father unpacked supplies from the canoe and I gathered kindling and small logs for the campfire. As the trout roasted over the open flame the three of us settled in for our midday meal and a bit of rest.

A Fateful Chain of Events

He had traveled north earlier that summer from Charleston, South Carolina, reaching Quebec City in late July. Meeting there with a group of southern sympathizers known as the "Southern Cross", a plan to sabotage the economic growth and stability of the northern states had been finalized. All the major industries, railroads, textile mills, and shipyards were deemed prime targets. Maine's lumber industry was a vital cog in that economy. His chosen assignment was to slow down and disrupt the booming logging industry in the northern Maine woods by reducing the flow of logs through Bangor, Maine, at that time the so-called lumber capital of the world.

Jean Raymond Brisebois was a descendant of a long-established lineage of French Huguenots who had fled to the English Colonies in 1685 after the revocation of the Edict of Nantes. Settling in the low country near Charleston, South Carolina, the family estate "Palmetto" was established by the family patriarch Jacques Cartier Brisebois. Located twenty-five miles up the Ashley River from Charleston, the estate had grown into a one-thousand-acre plantation worked by up to five hundred African slaves. Though the main commodity was rice, the reproduction of future African American slaves for the Charleston slave market brought in an enormous source of wealth to the family. Like the Laurens and Legarés of their region the Brisebois family was associated with the genteel lifestyle of the Southern planter elite.

Born on February 22, 1825, Jean Raymond had grown up in a society greatly influenced by the strong personalities and great events of the times. As a contemporary southern gentleman Brisebois exemplified the "dashing cavalier" of a vanishing age. Standing six feet four inches with black eyes, a mane of thick black wavy hair, and black trimmed goatee he stood out in a crowd. An expert marksman and horseman, he helped manage the ever-expanding estate of his forefathers with an energetic flair. Never married, his physical attractiveness and sense of chivalry endeared him to a host of southern belles, single and married, living in the lowlands region. Although liaisons with ladies of his social circle were not uncommon, he whetted his physical appetite with frequent late-night visits to the quarters of the female slaves under his charge. The Brisebois family was well known for the large number of mulatto slaves who ended up on the auction block.

His family's connections to the South Carolina planter elite molded his ideals and opinions from a young age. His father, Charles Auguste Brisebois,

A Fateful Chain of Events

was at the center of the fight against the controversial tariff of 1828, known in the South as the "Tariff of Abominations". Charles was among a group of leading South Carolinians who backed the political doctrine of nullification, introduced by South Carolina's leading national voice and then Vice-President of the United States John C. Calhoun. The South Carolina nullification crisis led to threats of secession, causing President Andrew Jackson to challenge the state with the use of federal force to uphold the nation's laws and even threatening to hang Calhoun for inciting treason. A compromise tariff bill, introduced by Jackson nemesis and nationalist Henry Clay, calmed the antagonists and averted a more serious crisis.

The conflict between states' rights and stronger federal authority would dominate national politics over the next thirty years. The growth of northern abolitionist sentiment championed in Congress by former President John Quincy Adams led many southern politicians to draw a line in the sand over the slavery issue. Jean Raymond Brisebois was so influenced by these southern ideals, entrenched in South Carolina politics, that he was later associated with the southern leadership identified as the "fire eaters". These men, conservative in nature, but radical to the extreme in their actions, steered the slave states closer and closer to the idea of permanent separation from the free states of the north and the dissolution of the Union.

In 1841, after ten years of private tutoring, Jean Raymond, at the age of sixteen, entered the Citadel, a nationally known military institution located in the heart of Charleston. His father Charles envisioned a future family connection and influence to the potential establishment of a southern military to protect the interests and rights of the southern states. Using the family's political power and economic clout, Charles hoped that a solid background and experience in military doctrine would elevate Jean Raymond into a future leadership role for the South.

The completion of Jean Raymond's mathematics study and military training at the Citadel coincided with the annexation of Texas and the inauguration of newly-elected dark horse Democrat James Knox Polk of Tennessee to the presidency in 1845. Influenced by the political legacy of "Old Hickory", fellow Tennessean and seventh president Andrew Jackson, Polk's campaign platform of U.S. expansion west, now called "Manifest Destiny", led to Polk's *nom de guerre* "Young Hickory".

The tension over Mexico's northern boundary with Texas escalated during the next year into what became known as the Mexican War when Mexican forces crossed the Rio Grande into territory claimed

A Fateful Chain of Events

by Texas. President Polk used this action as a threat to United States sovereignty and asked Congress for a declaration of war in 1846. Jean Raymond left the Citadel and entered the Corps of Engineers division of the United States Army as the fighting crossed the Rio Grande to Mexico and the conflict spread west to Mexican California. Jean Raymond's first assignment took him to New Orleans where he was attached to the staff of General Winfield Scott.

U.S. troops under General Zachary Taylor won key victories in northern Mexico at Buena Vista and Monterrey, allowing General Scott to organize his army for an invasion of Mexico and attack on Mexico City. This army, made up of regular and voluntary troops, was preparing for an amphibious landing at the coastal port of Vera Cruz and then a march to the Mexican capital. As part of the Corps of Engineers, Jean Raymond served under the immediate supervision of Captain Robert E. Lee of Virginia whose responsibility was to safely guide the U.S. forces through the inhospitable terrain as they marched toward Mexico City.

From Vera Cruz through Cerro Gordo, Churubusco, and the eventual surrender of a spent Mexican army at Chapultepec outside of Mexico City, Jean Raymond reveled in the thrill and jubilation of a decisive American victory. The resulting Treaty of Guadalupe Hidalgo ended the conflict and paved the way for the Mexican Cession. This agreement gave the United States control of all the Mexican territories stretching from the banks of the Rio Grande westward to the California coast. Along with the earlier Treaty of Oregon in 1846, "Manifest Destiny" was finally secured and southern Democrats, who had supported the war, envisioned a slave empire all the way to the Pacific Ocean.

The discovery of gold in California as the war was ending and the subsequent "Gold Rush" of 1849 escalated the population migration west and set the stage for California statehood and admittance to the Union. National leaders for the southern states' interests led by South Carolina's John C. Calhoun expressed support for the extension of slavery into the new territories of the Mexican Cession. When the citizens of California voted to abolish slavery and enter the Union as a free state, it caused a firestorm of controversy nationally, splitting North and South. The slave states again used the threat of secession from the Union if the expansion of slavery was not allowed to spread into the western territories. In the free states the growing abolitionist sentiment fueled the fire with calls to end the institution throughout the United States. When California applied for admittance to the Union as a free state both sides dug in their heels and the nation seemed on the verge of disintegration. In an unexpected move

A Fateful Chain of Events

President Zachary Taylor, a Mexican War hero and slave owner from Louisiana, opposed secession.

To resolve the crisis Senator Henry Clay of Kentucky proposed a set of bills that became known as the Compromise of 1850. President Taylor announced that he would not support the compromise as a concession to southern threats of secession and vowed to veto any compromise bills passed by Congress. During the compromise crisis Taylor became ill after a Fourth of July celebration and unexpectedly died. His successor, Vice President Millard Fillmore of New York, a supporter of the bills, signed the compromise legislation into law.

Along with California's admittance to the Union as a free state, the most controversial legislation was the passage of a stronger Fugitive Slave Law with federal enforcement to aid in the capture of runaway slaves. Northern opposition to abide by this new measure infuriated southerners and calls for secession of the southern slave states increased rapidly. To compound this rift, Harriet Beecher Stowe's novel, *Uncle Tom's Cabin*, depicting the cruelties of the slave system, sparked outrage. The genesis for the novel's theme occurred during discussions between Stowe's husband Calvin and his students. Calvin Stowe was a professor at Bowdoin College in Brunswick, Maine, where the antislavery sentiment was strong. The emotions raised over the novel's viewpoint ended any possibility of further compromise to solve the slavery crisis between the free northern states and slave southern states.

These contentious events were the impetus for Jean Raymond's increased politicalization. Although he never ran for office, Brisebois, like many planters of his era, had a keen interest in politics. A member of the Charleston Democrats, his mentor was the famed states' rights champion John C. Calhoun. With Calhoun's death shortly after the Compromise of 1850 crisis, Jean Raymond took a more prominent role in the Democrats' political philosophy and an increasing interest in the clandestine ideas that were floating around in political discussions. South Carolina and the other slave states needed to act quickly with force to save their way of life. As he entered his twenty-eighth year Jean Raymond was now prepared to take the radical steps needed to protect southern institutions and ideals.

To carry out these extreme ideas the more radical members of the Charleston Democrats formed a secret sect christened the "Cavaliers of the Confederacy". Their acts of espionage and terror would be assisted by southern sympathizers in New York City, Philadelphia, St. Louis, Cincinnati, Washington, D.C., and across the international border in Quebec City. With his ancestry and

A Fateful Chain of Events

command of the French language, Jean Raymond was a natural choice to work as an agent out of Quebec City.

Supported by agents in New York City his assignment was to disrupt the vital lumber industry in northern New England, focusing on the massive flow of timber moving through Bangor. He made several trips between Quebec and Bangor to survey the land and felt confident that his plans would meet with success. As he traveled the region posing as a Canadian lumberman, he made contact with many people associated with the timber industry—ax men, riggers, haulers, river men, timber scouts, and business men. He even spent time working in a lumber camp learning that the key to the entire process was the knowledge and information gathered by the timber scouts who traversed the Maine woods during the early fall season. He observed their daily operations and his plan was to disrupt the upcoming logging season by somehow sabotaging the reports the lumber companies received from the timber scouts. Jean Raymond was returning from a meeting with agents in New York when by chance he came across our party in Monson and he decided the time to act was now.

After our midday meal which consisted of the trout fried in salt pork, hard bread from a keg, and black tea sweetened with sugar to taste, we spent an hour dozing in the warmth of the noon day sun. As the hour passed my father was up and urging us to follow suit. After dousing the fire we loaded our gear back into the canoe to begin the next leg of our journey.

The wind had increased from the north to about fifteen knots causing some choppy waves. My father wanted to reach Farm Island, just to the north of Mt. Kineo by late afternoon to set up camp for the night. He estimated the distance to be about eight miles and the three of us put our backs into our paddling as we hugged the western shore heading north. As we passed the Moose River the height of Mt. Kineo towered before us to the northeast. To reach Farm Island we had to leave the relative safety of the shoreline for more rough and open water north northeast around the peninsula. Fighting a modest headwind of about twelve knots we eased our way through the strait which separated the western shore from the Kineo peninsula. We held our collective breaths as we traversed the choppy waters of the strait. That three-and-a-half-mile stretch to Farm Island seemed like an eternity as we maintained a steady pace to avoid being swamped by the relentless churning water. Reaching the southeast shore of Farm Island we eased the canoe through the rocks and found a landing spot with a sheltered glen ideal for setting up camp. With the

A Fateful Chain of Events

prospect of wet weather on the horizon we worked quickly to secure the canoe, unload our provisions, set up our tent, and gather dry wood to commence lighting the campfire. With these tasks completed we barely beat the wet weather that began to descend on our site. The shelter of the glen kept the provisions and ourselves relatively dry and we were able to feed the camp fire with little or no ill effects to the blaze. Setting up our tent with the open end to the leeward side gave us the advantage of tending the camp fire and preparing our dinner in relative comfort. For the evening meal we fried pork in the skillet, boiled rice in a pot, and brewed some more black tea to drink.

By the end of the meal the rain had stopped and while I took our utensils and pots to clean at the water's edge I stumbled across a large patch of wild raspberries that would be a welcome addition to our morning breakfast. I stored the berries in a safe place, stacked the utensils and pots near the fire to dry, and settled into my spot inside the tent. Although the storm had brought in cooler air, a full belly and the warmth of the campfire led me quickly to a deep slumber and sweet dreams of the good times I enjoyed with my friend Anne.

We arose before sunrise and rekindled the fire to ward off the chill and prepare breakfast. While I went down to the shoreline to fetch a pail of water for coffee and washing, Dexter commenced to cooking up breakfast, a mixture of cornmeal and molasses, molded into cakes and fried in the skillet. By the time I returned with the water my father had packed away the tent and Dexter had the griddle cakes laid out on plates to cool. While waiting for the coffee to brew we carried the tent and other gear down to where the canoe had been secured overnight and packed to save time before heading back to the fire for coffee, griddle cakes, and fresh berries.

Hot, strong black coffee balanced with the sweetness and crunch of the griddle cakes and tartness of the berries satisfied our appetites and fortified us for the day's travel that lay ahead. As the sun began to shine over the trees on the eastern shore we shoved off for the next leg of our journey, Northeast Carry, the portage at the head of Moosehead. The calmness of the early dawn allowed for easy and quick progress around the Kineo peninsula and along the northeastern shore of the lake. As we canoed across Moosehead the morning light revealed the presence of two large bull moose feeding in the shallows along the shore. As we passed they raised their heads and their massive antlers created a magnificent silhouette in the morning sunshine. We reached the head of the lake with no difficulties and landed at Northeast Carry. Pulling the canoe ashore, we stretched our limbs, and unpacked and divided the gear for the two-mile trek across the portage trail to the West Branch of the Penobscot River. Dexter and I overturned the canoe and tied our paddles to the bottom. Hoisting the canoe, Dexter placed it on his right shoulder, with an India rubber knapsack secured and strapped to his back. He also carried an India rubber bag in his left hand to help him balance out the heavy load. On the opposite side at the rear of the canoe I followed with the same burden. Leading the way up the portage, my father carried a large knapsack on his back and a rubber bag in each hand. As the sun shone high in the eastern sky we started across the rough portage to the West Branch. We stopped several times to rest as we trudged up the rugged Trail. It took us almost two hours to reach the Penobscot.

We took some time to rest at the river's edge, ate the griddle cakes and berries left over from breakfast, and washed down our food with the cold, clear water from the fast-flowing river. By the time we finished our respite and loaded the canoe, the sun was high in the southern sky. The West Branch at this point flows eastward for about two miles before sharply turning northeastward toward the upper end of Chesuncook Lake. At this time of the year the river current moves in an easy flow making traveling with the current a pleasant ride. My main responsibility on this stretch was to watch for any large rocks that might crop up along the river route. From the bend in the river we traveled ten miles downstream to Pine Stream Falls, a drop in the river which required us to make a short portage around, and then on for another five miles downriver to the northwest shore of Chesuncook Lake.

Our evening destination was Ansell Smith's farm, the center of civilization in this part of the Maine wilderness. It was a haven for the many lumbermen who worked the woods along the West Branch. As we paddled into the harbor to the shore there were half a dozen bateaux and four canoes nestled in among the stumps along the waterfront. Rising just above the harbor was an enormous log house at least eighty feet long. Walking down the slope from the log house to welcome us was a man I guessed to be Ansell Smith. He and my father, who had known each other since the Aroostook War of '39, greeted one another with a hearty and warm handshake. After introductions to Dexter and me by my father, we were led up the slope to the log house. Along with Smith and his family this spacious structure was a home and refuge of comfort to lumbermen and travelers alike. We were shown to one of the many sleeping quarters to stow our gear and wash up before the evening meal. The room was dry, clean, and comfortable with the sweet scent of fir which covered the floor. After settling and unpacking our gear my father took us on a short tour of the compound. The settlement had several buildings next to or near the log house spread around the large clearing. Among them were a cold cellar for storing food, a blacksmith shop where many tools were forged and repaired, and draft animals were shod. A large two-story barn that housed the animals and served as a storage for hay and equipment was an impressive structure. Near the barn was an enormous garden where many root vegetables were ready for harvesting. As we walked back toward the log house the dinner bell began to ring and the smell of fresh baked bread lured us on to the community dining hall.

As we entered the large hall we made our way among the long tables and benches to available seats located in the back. As many as thirty Yankee and Canadian lumbermen were also streaming in for the evening meal. Bits of conversation in both English and French interrupted by bursts of laughter filled the hall with a festive atmosphere. Our dinner was a hearty one, fresh-baked bread and churned butter, "bean hole'" baked beans with molasses and salt pork, a savory moose meat stew filled with potatoes, carrots, and turnip from the root garden, and topping off the meal a generous helping of warm deep-dish apple pie washed down with mugs of strong black coffee. As I looked about the hall, I caught a glimpse of what I thought was a familiar-looking face among the throng of boisterous lumbermen. The unexpected presence startled me momentarily and when I recovered from the shocking surprise and again surveyed the hall the familiar image had vanished into thin air. Sipping coffee as we finished our meal I mulled over and over in my mind how that moment of recognition could possibly have any connection to me or my family. As we left the dining hall a sudden light of reflection bore through the darkness and a possible answer came out of nowhere. Could this person be the French traveler who had joined us on the stagecoach ride from Monson to Greenville? As I searched the faces of the crowd of men exiting the dining hall I came up empty. With no hint of hard evidence to support my theory a sense of doubt crept into my head as we walked back to our lodgings.

My father left us to discuss plans with Ansell Smith for our scout up north the next day and to thank him for the generous hospitality given that evening. As Dexter and I walked toward our lodgings I stopped and asked him if he noticed anyone in the dining hall who had looked familiar to him. He said the food tasted so good that he hardly took his eyes off his plate. Completely lost in the joy of our delicious dinner he had paid no attention to the

A Fateful Chain of Events

other diners in the hall. When I told him who I thought I had recognized among the crowded faces in the hall but could not be sure of, he thought it was just a figment of my imagination because of the Frenchman's unusual manner and dress which seemed out of place in this part of Maine—it was just an odd coincidence and nothing more. Although Dexter's explanation seemed logical, for some reason deep down inside I still had a feeling of uneasiness. My father joined us shortly after we returned to our lodgings and told us we would be traveling at first light into the dense woods for three days of timber scouting along the shores of Chamberlain Lake, located about fifteen miles to the north.

Before the crack of dawn we were up, and after quietly packing our gear, gathered our bundles and left the lodgings. To our surprise the Smiths had prepared an early morning breakfast of baked beans, fresh biscuits, strawberry preserves, and strong black coffee. After enjoying this unexpected surprise to begin our day we thanked the Smiths and headed down the embankment to our canoe. Ansell used a lantern to guide us down to the shoreline and after loading the canoe we bid him a good day. As we shoved out into the darkness of the lake we could barely make out the faint rays of the early morning sunrise although the dim light helped us navigate back to the head of Chesuncook's western shore.

Steering the canoe north from the lake we entered the outlet of the Umbazookskus Stream. This was the first time since we entered the West Branch at Northeast Carry that the current flowed against us. Umbazookskus is an Indian name meaning "much meadow river". The name aptly described the scene before us. The rising sun, now just above the eastern tree line, slowly revealed a wide expanse of dark meadowy water between the woods that hugged the border on either side of the stream. The slowness of the water current offered little resistance as we paddled north toward the stream's outlet, Umbazookskus Lake. The five-mile trip to the lake was an enjoyable and serene paddle as we easily made our way upstream. The chirping sounds of the olive-sided flycatcher and sweet songs of the red-breasted robin serenaded us along the way and for a brief moment brought me back to our recent traveling companion Thoreau. He would have been in his glory describing the birds and their habitat. The sun was now above the eastern tree line and the wilderness was wide awake with nature's activity. About two miles upstream we caught sight of a pair of hawks out for an early morning hunt. One of the hawks swooped through the air and went into a dive at the edge of the woods. After losing sight of the bird briefly, I saw it suddenly fly out of the trees clutching a small rabbit and then fly north toward the lake, the

A Fateful Chain of Events

other hawk following close behind. We kept a sharp lookout for a nest in the trees as we neared the lake but saw no signs of one. At this point the stream narrowed, the current gained strength, and the woods, mostly larch trees, closed in. As we entered the lake it proved to be quite rocky and shallow below the surface. Paddling with caution we made our way across to the eastern shore. My father directed us to a small clearing in the woods surrounding Umbazookskus Lake and we gently landed on the rocky shore. This was the start of our next portage that would take us across the trail to Mud Pond which was our connection to Chamberlain Lake. The forest at our landing point hugged the shoreline leaving little room for dry ground. We unloaded the canoe near the trail and organized our baggage for the carry ahead.

Before starting across the portage it was time to rest and eat so I gathered some kindling and cut short tree limbs to start a small campfire. As I brewed some tea Dexter unpacked the skillet, pork, and hard bread from the barrels and started to prepare our midday meal. We also added beans and rice from the Smith farm after the pork was fried. In the meantime, my father walked up the portage trail to scout the conditions for our carry. Dexter was just finishing frying the pork and the tea was ready when my father returned with bad news. The trail was very wet on this end with slippery footing that would make the portage a more difficult trek. He also reported that just up the trail about a half a mile was a small log hut which was occupied by a Canadian family, the Thurlottes, who had lived there for over a year. It was a tough spot to try and establish a homestead and the family, which included four children, were quite downtrodden. He felt guilty that we had only a few provisions to share with the family on our way by. Already tuckered out we fortified ourselves for the difficult task at hand while eating in silence. After dinner I doused the fire while Dexter put aside the rest of the pork, rice, beans and bread along with a fair amount of black tea as an offering to the family when we reached the hut near the trail. We organized our gear in preparation for the next leg of our journey to Chamberlain Lake.

As had been the case with our Northeast Carry portage, Dexter and I shouldered the canoe and followed my father up the trail. It was slow going as the wet conditions made the footing treacherous. More than once Dexter or I stumbled and the fear of going down hard made us extra cautious. My father estimated the carry to Mud Pond was just under two miles but it seemed like an eternity as we crawled along at a snail's pace. Despite the atrocious conditions the trail was a main route and was free of blow downs and other obstacles common to the

A Fateful Chain of Events

woods and we were able to maintain a slow but steady pace. When we reached the hut of the Thurlotte family we stopped to catch our breaths and offer them the meager rations Dexter had packed. The family's plight gave me a hollow feeling as I viewed the desperate life they were living here in the Maine wilderness. Their heartfelt words of gratitude for our offering touched me, especially the faces of the children, and I felt guilty as we bade them goodbye and continued up the trail. After two hours of hard travel with frequent stops we reached the gloomy shores of Mud Pond. Looking across to the opposite shore from the end of our portage the name Mud Pond fit this body of water to a tee. The small pond, coffee color in tint, contained much more mud than pond water. It just seemed to be a wetter version of the portage we had just traversed. As we stopped to rest for a bit my father drew our attention to an opening in the trees along the northern shore where a stream entered the pond about a mile across from the portage. He told us that this was the connection that would lead us to Chamberlain Lake. Not wanting to linger too long on that wet and now buggy shoreline, we loaded the canoe and headed across the pond to the outlet. The pond was just barely deep enough to keep our full canoe afloat though our paddles constantly touched the muddy bottom. The water proved a bit deeper at the entrance to the outlet and we pushed into the slow-moving current where we were engulfed by a swarm of bugs and the heavy tree growth of the forest. Twice, while fighting off the annoying bugs, we had to get out into the thigh-deep stream to pull the canoe over the blow downs that blocked the passage. After getting over the second blow down the current quickened and the water became deeper as we paddled out of the heavy growth of trees into a small open bay. The uncomfortable closeness of the air we had felt during the portage and crossing the pond and into the stream was suddenly replaced by the cool freshness of a slight northern breeze which blew across the open bay. The fresh air carried with it the scent of sweet northern pine and that aroma invigorated and shook us from the lethargy that had overcome us in the stale and heavy air of the portage and Mud Pond. Once out into the bay my father guided us to the north and west where another small outlet was our connection to Chamberlain Lake.

The narrow passage from the bay brought us on to the lake and leaving the bay outlet we paddled west along the southern shoreline to a gravely and rock-strewn peninsula about midway along the large lake. The peninsula tree line set back away from the water and numerous gray weathered logs were scattered about. This was at the northern fringe of logging operations in the Maine woods during that time. We set up camp among the logs and after unpacking and securing the canoe we waded into the lake to wash off the mud caked to our clothes and our bodies. After our refreshing dip we hung our clothes to dry among the branches of the fallen logs and built a fire to help with the drying, as well as to provide us some warmth, and to start cooking our evening meal. About a mile and a half across the lake in a clearing along the northern shore was the Chamberlain Farm which stood out against the backdrop of a deep dark green forest that towered beyond. Consisting of three large log buildings, my father pointed out that it was the supply depot for the lumbermen working in the woods along Chamberlain Lake and farther north about five miles away at Eagle Lake. This was to be the area of concentration my father would scout to gather information for the lumber company back in Bangor.

The smoke from our fire brought activity from the opposite shore and in no time a canoe appeared on the lake, paddled by two men and heading towards our camp site. We boiled a large pot of tea and unpacked extra cups for the arrival of our approaching guests. They glided ashore about three quarters of an hour later and as we walked down to greet them one of the men held up a huge mess of fresh trout. My father stepped immediately toward the man and they shook hands and slapped backs warmly. He was introduced to Dexter and me as Joe and as the other man came up from the canoe Joe introduced us to Pierre. Joe and Pierre were working as hired caretakers of the supply depot and the smoke from our campfire was their signal to paddle over as official greeters. While my father and I talked "timber" with our guests, Dexter cleaned the trout, six plump foot-long beauties, and had them frying in the skillet in a matter of minutes. After a sumptuous repast of fresh trout, hard bread, and tea our guests lingered long enough after dinner to smoke tobacco from their corn cob pipes and visit. They proved to be genial guests and excellent company. As daylight began to fade in the western sky we exchanged thanks—us for the feast of trout and them for the bread and tea. Saying our goodbyes for the evening we watched them slowly paddle back across the lake as the dusk quickly descended into darkness and they faded out of sight. My father was very pleased with the information Joe and Pierre had provided and planned out a two-day scout that would take us from the shore of the Chamberlain Farm north to the southern shore of Eagle Lake. After cleaning up our dinner plates and utensils and organizing my bags for tomorrow's early morning start I settled in for a comfortable and restful night's sleep. Lying out in the open with clean, dry clothes and a full belly I enjoyed the magnificent display of stars across the

A Fateful Chain of Events

clear dark autumn sky for a short time before falling into a very fitful sleep.

Waking to the lonely cry of a loon and the smell of freshly-brewed coffee, I rolled over to see Dexter and my father already up and standing by a low campfire which cast them in silhouette against the hour's darkness. Dexter's cornmeal and molasses cakes were sizzling in the skillet and a plate of steaming fried pork was cooling on a nearby rock. The early morning daylight was just beginning to overtake the darkness in the eastern sky as I arose and stretched to start a brand-new day. After neatly packing my bed roll I walked to the water's edge to wash the sleep from my eyes with a splash of cool water from the lake. Dexter's cakes were ready to eat and approaching the fire he handed me a large mug of black coffee. My father said today we could enjoy a leisurely breakfast before canoeing across the lake to the farm. A second cup of coffee, along with the pork and griddle cakes energized me for the day ahead and I savored the moment. As we washed our pans, plates, and utensils at the water's edge, a flock of loons, three adults and six chicks, came gliding across the lake just in front of me. The lead loon was occasionally diving under the surface and reappearing farther out as they swam away from the shoreline. Two moose, a bull and a cow, were casually feeding in the reeds along the western shore and stopped for a short time to watch the train of loons as well before resuming their breakfast. As the sun rose in the eastern sky we broke camp and packed up the canoe before shoving off towards the Chamberlain Farm. The first leg across the lake was smooth and easy, but as the sun rose higher and heated the air the water became quite choppy as we reached the middle of the lake. We slowed our pace and cautiously paddled to the northern shore reaching the landing at the Chamberlain Farm about an hour after breaking camp.

We secured the canoe to a tall pine tree and loaded our packs for the two-day scout. Hailing the caretakers, we neither saw nor heard any sign of Joe and Pierre as we approached the main building. My father thought they might have gone out for an early morning moose hunt over on the western side of the lake. Walking eastward along the shore from the depot we quickly came upon a well-worn trail and plunged into the cool shade of the thick woods. Unlike our travails along Mud Pond we were luckily spared the nuisance of swarms of bugs and except for an occasional swat to rid a lone pest we proceeded deep into the forest with relative comfort. As we started up the trail, the stillness of the wilderness was abruptly shattered by the sound of two successive gun shots to the west. We had no doubt they came from Joe and Pierre and knew that

A Fateful Chain of Events

their expert shooting meant a successful hunt and the prize of a fresh supply of savory moose meat for their dinner table. My father's task was to compile information as to the abundance of white pine ready for cutting in the upcoming logging season. He was especially scouting for the "King's Pines", those tall straight trees that had been restricted to crown use during colonial times in North America and now sought worldwide. About a half a mile into the woods we veered off the trail and into the thick of the forest where my father's knowledge and skill were put on full display. His instincts in the wilderness astounded me!

Over the next two days we traipsed through the heart of the dense Maine forest. With Dexter's and my assistance my father took numerous measurements and notes to compile the most accurate information he could decipher for the lumbermen. These detailed observations would be vital to the logging company in Bangor as they prepared and planned for the timber season. Our scout took us from the middle of Chamberlain's northern shore back northwest near the southern shores of Eagle Lake. There we connected back to the trail leading to Chamberlain Lake called the Eagle Lake Road. Our first night out we endured a long and heavy autumn rain storm which not only came with torrential downpours but also produced strong wind gusts which caused the trees to careen dangerously. Fortunately, we had been forewarned by the sounds of the high winds and the sudden darkness of the western sky. Pitching the tent facing toward the leeward side of the storm gave us more than ample protection and though we were unable to make a campfire during the night our baggage and ourselves remained relatively dry. As nighttime advanced and the storm slowly subsided we supped on berries collected during the day's scout and drank water collected at a cold brook crossed earlier that day. Eventually, due to our day's labors, we drifted into a relatively calm and comfortable sleep as the sounds of the storm echoed farther to the east.

Rising in the morning to clear, cooler air and a moderate northwest wind, we surveyed the effects of the previous night's storm. Along with the dampness many small trees and large branches had fallen down all around us. Dexter used some dry kindling he collected the day before to start our campfire and we brewed a large pot of strong coffee to start the new day. After coffee we broke camp, resuming the scout in the direction of Eagle Lake. About midday, after a difficult morning navigating around many blow downs and gathering more information, we reached the southern shore of Eagle Lake. This was at the northernmost boundary of our timber scout. While we rested we ate the rest of the berries and took in the view looking across Eagle Lake and the wild beauty of the northern Maine wilderness in the late autumn afternoon. My father used our rest time to enter his final information into the logbook and after a twenty-minute break he was ready to travel again, wanting to reach the depot before dark. The Eagle Lake Road headed south about five miles to the Chamberlain Farm and proved to be fairly smooth and, in spite of the recent heavy rain, a relatively dry route. Although five large pine trees had blown down during the storm and blocked the trail we easily climbed over the obstacles and made good time, reaching the northern shore of Chamberlain Lake by late that afternoon.

Pierre was roasting a large haunch of moose meat over a huge fire pit just outside the main depot building. Approaching the compound Joe hailed us with a hearty greeting as we emerged from the woods. After we shook hands and re-acquainted ourselves they offered us hot tea and freshly baked bread from the wood oven. Ravished from our day's efforts in the woods and the meager amount of food eaten we lost little time in digging into their generous offering. As we rested by the fire pit sipping hot tea my father shared his new scouting information with the two caretakers.

The answers from Joe and Pierre to his questions concerning his scouting information made him confident that his observations were on a par with those of these two experienced woodsmen. Satisfied, he relaxed and looked quite pleased and content as we enjoyed their camp camaraderie. Finally, after over an hour of smelling the aroma of roasted meat, Pierre announced to us that the moose meat was ready to eat and he began to slice off large, juicy chunks, crispy brown on the outside and pink on the inside. As the meat from the haunch rested on a large platter he surprised us by digging out ten large potatoes that had been roasting under the coals at the side of the fire pit. Added to the roasted meat they provided a hearty and delicious feast along with more fresh bread and hot tea. After supper we sat around the fire pit as Joe and Pierre regaled us with their tales of native lore from the great north woods describing how the great spirit "Glooscap" created the Penobscot River by killing a greedy toad who had swallowed all the water in their homeland and then taking the mud from the banks of the river to create humans. They also recalled the legend of the powerful chief named Kineo who was banished to the mountain by his own people for the harsh and cruel leadership he imposed on the tribe. After his death the mountain became a common gathering place for the region's people who were attracted to the site due to its abundance of rhyolite, commonly known as flint, from which the people made their arrow and spear heads. Hearing the legends of the first people to live in Maine gave me a sense of kinship as a fellow traveler through those now sacred places and we broke up our community campfire just before sunset.

My father wanted to use the remaining daylight to cross Chamberlain to its southern shore for an early start southward to Ansell Smith's farm. Saying goodbye to our gracious hosts we loaded our canoe and shoved off into the calmness of the lake. The crossing proved peaceful and easy with a slight tail wind from the northwest aiding our efforts. We arrived along the southern shore at our previous camp site just as the sun set behind the trees along the western shore. With the moon rising in the darkening eastern sky and the prospect of a clear and comfortable night ahead we crawled into our bedrolls under an open starlit sky.

My father woke us before sunrise the next morning. A small campfire glowed and the smell of brewing coffee filled the cool morning air. Along with our coffee we enjoyed a special treat given to us by Joe and Pierre. We had a half dozen slices of roasted moose meat to eat with our coffee and fortify us for the day's travel ahead. My father's goal was to reach the Ansell Smith farm by late afternoon and after a night's rest push east down Chesuncook Lake. From the eastern shore of the lake a short portage around the falls at Ripogenus Gorge would take us to the West Branch of the Penobscot the following day. Dousing the fire, we packed the canoe and paddled toward the outlet taking us to Mud Pond. Although I quietly dreaded the thought of making that passage back through the portage to Umbazookskus Lake I was driven by the promise of a comfortable night along the shores of Chesuncook. The early dawn provided just enough light to navigate the narrow water passage and by the time we reached Mud Pond the sun was beginning to shine brightly above the eastern forest. Not wanting to linger longer than necessary, we unloaded the canoe and began our trek from Mud Pond. Due to the recent heavy rain the portage across to Umbazookskus Lake was much more treacherous than our earlier carry from the south. By the mid-morning we reached the forlorn cabin along the portage and stopped briefly to offer those poor souls two slices of moose meat left over from our breakfast. The gratitude shown was heartwarming. We reached the end of the portage at the northern shore of the lake and took time out to once again wash the mud from our clothes and bodies covering us from head to toe. The water felt quite cold so we didn't linger too long. Laying our wet clothes out on the flat rocks and sitting in the bright sunshine helped to dry our clothes and provided much needed warmth. Dexter made a small fire and

A Fateful Chain of Events

brewed some tea which gave us an added feeling of warmth. The hot tea was very soothing and with the fire's heat aided in bringing much-needed relaxation and removed much of the tension I had felt during the portage. In about an hour the canoe was loaded and we were paddling across the lake and entering the Umbazookskus Stream flowing at our backs to the south. With the current in our favor we made good time to the northeastern entrance of the stream into Chesuncook. Paddling into the lake we came in full view of Ansell Smith's farm which was set upon the large clearing to the south. We paddled into the harbor at about 3:00 p.m. which was right on my father's mid-afternoon time table and easily found a landing spot where we nestled the canoe between the always crowded array of bateaux and canoes that were neatly lined up along the shore. Gliding ashore we pulled the canoe up between the stumps, unpacked our gear, and headed up to the large log house where Ansell Smith was just emerging through the front door.

After a friendly greeting Dexter and I carried all our baggage to the lodgings we had occupied on our earlier visit while Ansell and my father went inside to talk about the conditions to the north and to discuss my father's notes compiled during the timber scout. As we made our way to the sleeping compartment I kept a watchful eye out in the hopes of seeing that familiar face that had surprised me in the dining hall the week before. There were many men about working in the blacksmith shop, some splitting and stacking firewood, or tending to the last remnants of the large root garden near the barn but no one we encountered looked familiar. After unpacking our bed rolls Dexter and I sat outside the lodging on a wooden bench and enjoyed the last rays of the sun on a spectacular autumn day. As the sun slowly faded in the western sky I sat and reflected on all my father had accomplished in his life, caring son, loving and faithful husband, affectionate father, respected businessman, skilled woodsman, and hoped I could live up to those high standards and come close to his many successes. My father returned and told us Ansell estimated that we could reach Bangor from the farm in two or three days' travel if the present fair weather held. My father would turn in his information at the lumber office and then we would catch the steamer at the docks for the trip down the Penobscot to the bay and home. That would put us back in Rockland by September 28, giving me two weeks before I returned to school to start the fall session. I hoped to use that time for my own pleasure if my father would consent to freeing me up from my shipyard chores. As I mulled over how to approach him on that subject the dinner bell rang and the three of us headed for the dining

A Fateful Chain of Events

hall, following the aroma of roasted meat and vegetables that filled the cool evening air. My eyes darted to and fro as I watched the crowd of men entering the hall hoping to catch a glimpse of that familiar face that still haunted me, but alas, to no avail.

Finding room on a bench close to where we sat on our previous stay I had a full view of the hall and constantly scanned the crowd of diners as we talked and ate. The table was set with baskets of fresh baked bread and churned sweet butter along with a surprising treat, cups of sweet cider pressed from juicy MacIntosh apples picked from the Smith farm's orchard. While enjoying the bread, butter, and cider we joined in the conversation with the diners around us about the great fall weather and what changes were expected in the upcoming logging season. The men seemed quite anxious for the ground to harden and the snow to start falling, which signaled the start of the cutting season that would last through the spring thaw. As we listened platters of roast pork and root vegetables began to appear on the tables and the noisy chatter disappeared as we filled our plates and devoured the main course. Topping off the meal were large slices of warm apple pie that we washed down with mugs of piping hot black coffee. After we finished our delicious dinner we wished our fellow diners a successful season and as we left the dining hall I scanned the crowd for that all-too-familiar but mysterious face, again coming up empty. This seemed to satisfy my curiosity and I finally put the matter to rest once and for all. As usual my father was itching to get an early start and we immediately retired to our lodgings for a cozy and comfortable night's sleep. As I drifted off my thoughts turned as always to Anne and I wished there was some way I could travel to Brunswick for a visit before the new school session started. That dream seemed far out of reach.

    We were awake before dawn and after packing our bed rolls and gathering our packs we made our way down to the canoe. The early morning had not yet dawned and after securing our baggage we headed for the dining hall where the Smiths had fresh brewed coffee, bread and raspberry preserves, and smoked sausage with eggs set out on the table. My father said the breakfast feast would tide us over for the entire day and the hours we gained would bring extra travel time before dusk overtook us. After thanking the Smiths again for their hospitality, we walked to the shore in the company of Ansell and bid a final farewell as we shoved out into the lake and paddled toward the east as the sky began to brighten overhead. We settled in to enjoy what we hoped would be an easy paddle down the Chesuncook to the West Branch of the Penobscot, my father in the

A Fateful Chain of Events

stern, Dexter in the middle, and me in the bow. Our only portage would be the trail around Ripogenus Gorge, a dangerous stretch of whitewater and falls that was the outlet from the lake to the river. With a slight tail wind to aid us and calm waters on the lake we basked in the warmth of the rising sun paddling at a smooth and steady pace along the southern shore of Chesuncook as the surrounding forest slowly came to life in the early morning sunlight. The sound and activity coming from the wilderness was all around us as we made our way eastward. Hawks hovered overhead ready to swoop down on any unsuspected prey, a flock of loons dove for fish in the middle of the lake, a bull moose slowly chewed as he enjoyed his breakfast among the reeds, and further down three deer, a buck and two does, were quietly drinking from the mouth of a small stream along the shoreline. As the full sunshine rapidly appeared overhead and warmed the chill of the morning air it seemed as if nothing could interrupt this moment of serene beauty. After paddling about fifteen miles we approached the beginnings of the swifter current leading to Ripogenus Gorge and my father began to steer us closer to the southern shore to avoid the whitewater and prepare for the portage around the falls.

In Search of Honor

* * *

He knew the young man, Benjamin, had seen him among the crowd eating in the dining hall. Quickly and without drawing attention Jean Raymond Brisebois slipped out the door and into the darkness. Waiting in the shadows he watched the young man, his father, and friend leave the hall. He hoped young Benjamin had not recognized him and cause his true identity and presence at the farm to come into question, exposing his plans. Staying out of sight to avoid any risk, Brisebois spent a long sleepless night watching and waiting. When the Dean party emerged from their lodgings early the next morning he followed them closely from the shadows and learned of their departure for the Chamberlain Farm to scout timber and expected return in three days' time. Breathing a sigh of relief as they paddled north he began to hatch his plan. Brisebois, along with three French Canadian sympathizers, had spent the past six months working on and off at the Smith farm and had become familiar with the lay of the land around Chesuncook during their travels. Using that knowledge Brisebois hoped to deal a sharp blow to the operations of the vital lumber industry. Choosing the right place and time would be crucial to his success.

A Fateful Chain of Events

* * *

As we slowly drifted towards the shoreline our peaceful ride quickly turned into a race for survival. Suddenly, from behind a peninsula on the northern shore, a bateau carrying four men appeared out of nowhere on the lake. It was moving swiftly across the water with the first three men paddling furiously towards us on a steady collision course, and the fourth man, sitting in the stern, was guiding the bateau toward our canoe while he barked out urgent commands in French. As the bateau rapidly approached, the face of the man in the stern came into full view. To my shocked surprise it was the familiar face I had glimpsed in the dining hall earlier in the week. As they began to quickly overtake us I realized the man in the stern was definitely that of the French traveler Jean Raymond Brisebois whom we had met on the stagecoach from Monson to Greenville. At that moment his face looked sinister, with an expression of evil intent as he desperately called to his oarsmen to overtake and cut us off.

By this time we were well into the swift current of the gorge, vainly struggling to free ourselves from the treacherous whitewater and reach the safety of the southern shore. With the bateau just off our port side there seemed to be no escape. As I continued to paddle furiously at an angle toward the shore my father and Dexter prepared to take on our attackers. The heavy bateau struck the port stern and jarred us with such force that our canoe almost overturned. Raymond made a lunge at my father, falling on top of him in the stern of the canoe just as Dexter was standing up to fight off two of the three oarsmen and I continued to paddle with all my might towards the southern shoreline. The suddenness of Raymond's desperate move caused Dexter to lose his balance and topple overboard. As I reached out to grab him the weight of his fall surprised me and I was pulled out of the canoe as well. Plunging into the water unexpectedly, I kicked hard to escape the danger of the strong current and reach shallow water. As I came to the surface I saw our canoe spinning and rapidly heading for the outlet to the gorge, pulled by the force of the whitewater. At that moment Dexter emerged to the surface next to me. Frantically searching for my father I saw the bateau struggling to escape the deadly current. The oarsmen were expending every ounce of their strength to reach the opposite shore. It was at that moment as the bateau turned around to the port side that I saw my father clinging to the side of their boat and struggling with the Frenchman who was back in the bateau's stern. Overcome by fear and rage I attempted to swim out to my father's aid but Dexter grabbed my arms and using his strength pulled me towards the shore as I struggled to free myself. Standing in the shallow water we watched in horror as the Frenchman struck my father on top of his head with the blade of an oar and he disappeared rapidly under the swift current of the whitewater, never to resurface. For a few seconds we both stood frozen in stunned silence while the scene unfolded before our eyes. Then suddenly, in a vain attempt to save my father, I tried again to swim out into the deadly current. As before, Dexter's strong grip and sensible words stopped my rather desperate and reckless actions. As I could find no sign of my father, reality finally overtook me and my body went limp with defeat and the sickening feeling of total remorse. Sitting on a rock in the shallow water near Ripogenus Gorge I went into a state of utter shock and numbness at the loss of my heroic and courageous father. Dexter came over, and putting a hand on my shoulder, helped me on to dry ground. It would be a long and sad walk of fifteen miles back up the southern shore of Chesuncook to Ansell Smith's farm. Looking back and gazing one more time across the churning water I prayed for justice as the four men in the bateau landed on the opposite shore and quickly disappeared into the empty darkness of the Maine wilderness.

Epilogue

The memory of that tragic day near Ripogenus Gorge has brought an overwhelming sense of sadness and heartache that has remained everlasting. The strength of my family in the hour of the devastating loss of our father had allowed me to slowly recover my purpose and the need to move forward with my life. My dear mother, our greatest source of strength and inspiration, urged me to work hard to pursue a meaningful and honored goal for the future. In the aftermath of our father's tragic and sudden death my brother Sam assumed the burden of the daily operations of the Dean shipyard and with the expert help and guidance of the ever-faithful Dexter Barrows continued the family business in a tradition of excellence along the mid coast. My sister Carrie's stout heart, moral character, and splendid companionship set an example for me to follow in that time of great sorrow. The resilience and stoic calm of my grandparents, Oliver and Martha, helped to mend my broken heart and soothe my guilt over our loss. When days proved difficult I looked to my father's example to forge ahead. Over the next few years, due to my family's unwavering support, I regained much of the positive outlook on life that had always been a part of my nature.

Sources

1. Banks, Ronald F.; *Maine Becomes a State. The Movement to Separate Maine From Massachusetts,* 1785-1820; New Hampshire Publishing Company; Somersworth, 1973.

2. Clark, Charles E.; W.W. Norton & Company, Inc.; New York, 1977.

3. Eaton, Cyrus; *History of Thomaston, Rockland, and South Thomaston, Maine, from their first exploration,* A.D. 1605, Vol. I; Masters, Smith & Company, Printers; Hallowell, 1865.

4. Eckstrom, Fannie Hardy; *The Penobscot Man*; Jordan-Frost Printing Company; Bangor, 1931.

5. Harden, Brian R.; *Shore Village Story—An Informal History of Rockland, Maine*; Courier-Gazette, Inc.; Rockland, 1976

6. Hawthorne-Longfellow Library; Collections, Primary Sources: Joshua Lawrence Chamberlain; Brunswick, Maine

7. Locke, John L.; *Sketches of The History of The Town of Camden, Maine; Including Incidental References to The Neighboring Places and Adjacent*

Waters; Masters, Smith, & Company; Hallowell, 1859.

8. Rowe, William Hutchinson; *The Maritime History of Maine, Three Centuries of Shipbuilding and Seafaring*; W.W. Norton and Company; New York, 1948.

9. Thoreau, Henry David; *The Maine Woods*, notes by Dudley C. Lunt; W.W. Norton & Company; New York, 1950.

10. Trulock, Alice Rains; *In the Hands of Providence: Joshua Chamberlain and The American Civil War*, The University of North Carolina Press; Chapel Hill, 1992.

11. Wallace, Willard; *Soul of The Lion, A Biography of General Joshua L. Chamberlain*; Thomas Nelson & Sons; New York, 1960.

About the Author

The author is a retired history teacher from Rockland, where he, his wife Darcy, son Ben, and daughter Carrie lived for several years. He and his wife currently reside in Portland with their pet cat Morris.

www.ingramcontent.com/pod-product-compliance
Lightning Source LLC
LaVergne TN
LVHW011427080426
835512LV00005B/306